NOTE ON THE
HISTORICAL RESULTS
DEDUCIBLE FROM RECENT
DISCOVERIES IN AFGHANISTAN

NOTE ON THE
HISTORICAL RESULTS
DEDUCIBLE FROM RECENT
DISCOVERIES IN AFGHANISTAN

BY

H. T. PRINSEP, ESQ.

GYAN

Published by

GYAN

Gyan Publishing House
5, Ansari Road
Daryaganj, New Delhi-110002
Phone: 011-47034999, 9811692060
E-mail: books@gyanbooks.com

Distribution Network
gyanbooks.com
India, USA, Canada, UK, Australia, France

ISBN : 978-81-212-2564-9 (HB)
First Published, 1844

2nd Impression 2021

Printed at: Gyan Press, Delhi.

Note on the
Historical Results Deducible from Recent Discoveries in Afghanistan
Author: H. T. Prinsep

NOTE ON THE HISTORICAL RESULTS,

DEDUCIBLE FROM RECENT

DISCOVERIES IN AFGHANISTAN.

BY

H. T. PRINSEP, Esq.

LONDON:

Wm. H. ALLEN AND CO.,

7, LEADENHALL STREET.

1844.

PREFACE.

The Public are not unacquainted with the fact, that discoveries of much interest have recently been made in the regions of Central Asia, which were the seat of Greek dominion for some hundred years after their conquest by Alexander. These discoveries are principally, but not entirely, numismatic, and have revealed the names of sovereigns of Greek race, and of their Scythian, and Parthian successors, of none of whom is any mention to be found in the extant histories of the East or West. There has also been opened to the curious, through these coins, a language, the existence of which was hitherto unknown, and which must have been the vernacular dialect of some of the regions in which the Grecian colonies were established. The coins possess particular value as a key for the cypher of this language through their bilingual legends and superscriptions, and have been extensively and successfully used for that purpose. But the investigation deserves, and requires to be further prosecuted, for there are inscriptions forthcoming in the language, which, if the ingenuity of the learned should succeed in completely translating and explaining them, cannot fail to throw much light, on the worse than Cimmerian darkness, that still envelops the age and country which have bequeathed them to us.

Amongst the earliest of those who directed public attention to these bilingual coins, and the most successful interpreter of their legends, was the late Mr. James Prinsep, Secretary of the Asiatic Society of Calcutta, and Editor of the Society's Journal, published monthly in that city. In both capacities he was naturally placed in direct and constant communication with those engaged in the work of practical discovery; and the assistance and instruction he was thus enabled to give, and readily and freely imparted to those, who, by the accident of position, were led to prosecute such researches, or who, by other means, became possessed of objects of antiquarian curiosity, was so frequently acknowledged by the gift of the articles discovered, that a very rich and extensive cabinet was the fruit. As an instance of the oriental liberality with which these things were presented, it may be stated, that, consequently upon a favorable mention in the Journal, of Gen. Ventura's researches at Manikyala, the vases, coins, and relics, found in the tope opened there in 1830, were freely and gratuitously given to the Editor by the General, and duplicates of his large assortment of Greco-Bactrian coins were similarly presented, in consideration of some little pains bestowed on the reading and classification of the more complete set, which the General made up to be forwarded to France.

Mr. James Prinsep, unfortunately, died before the investigation into the results of these discoveries had reached that point, which would warrant a satisfactory classification and arrangement of the articles he so obtained. The cabinet thus came to his widow, rich and various, but unsorted, and uncatalogued. In this condition, she applied to the Author of the following pages for advice and assistance as to its disposal; and he in consequence, as well as from a sense of duty, as for an agreeable and profitable occupation, undertook its arrangement, referring for that purpose to modern works written on the subject, and seeking in history, and in classic literature, for information regarding the period to which the coins and relics belonged.

Along with the cabinet, the note-book of the deceased was placed in the Author's hands; and it is the possession of that, and of the plates prepared originally for the Journal, and still fortunately preserved, that has led the Author to think, that it will be beneficial to put together, in the brief form adopted in these pages, the results deducible from recent discoveries. The free use of his brother's materials will, it is conceived, give the work a value, even with the most erudite; but its principal aim is, to place, in a cheap and commodious form before the popular reader, the means of gratifying curiosity upon a subject often referred to, and of the existence of which, as a successful result of modern research, few are entirely ignorant.

If the following pages shall have the effect of communicating information to readers, who have hitherto been deterred by the learning, or by the cost of the more elaborate works which have appeared, and so should stimulate curiosity, and excite a wider interest in respect to these discoveries, the Author's object will be gained. The present Note is confined to Bactro-Arian relics, but the late Mr. James Prinsep's cabinet is richer far in coins of India, Boodhist, and Brahminical, extending from periods of the most remote antiquity to the date of Mahomedan conquest; and for these a separate study, and if the subject be of sufficient general interest, a separate Note of explanation may be required.

LIST OF PLATES.

ERRATA.

PAGE

7. Seventh line from bottom, *dele* "All."
18. Eleventh line from bottom, *for* "its" *read* "the."
34. Fifth line, Date of Mithridates II. *for* B.C. 115 *read* B.C. 125.
38. Fourth line of Note, *for* "Judiasm" *read* "Judaism."
42. Fifteenth line, *for* "Bulkh" *read* "Hormuz."
57. Fifth line from bottom, *for* "on" *read* "or."

HISTORICAL RESULTS, &c.

Aria, Ariana, Bactria. These are names that every one has met with in the course of his reading, but very few know the precise locality of the regions so called,* and fewer still their history. The ancient authors of Greece and Rome furnish only some stray notices of kings who have conquered and reigned in those countries; but neither kings nor kingdoms are ever mentioned, except incidentally because of their coming in contact with nations of the West; and we seek in vain for any consistent account of the dynasties which rose and fell, or even of the races that came and went, conquering and conquered, during the thousand years that followed the conquest and settlement of

* Aria is the territory of which Herat is the Capital. Ariana (Eeran) is the general name for the country east of Persia and Media, as far as the Indus. Bactria is the country watered by the Oxus and its tributaries. Soghdiana the mountains which feed the Jaxartes, and divide the two rivers.

these regions by Alexander of Macedon, the son of Philip.

We know, indeed, that for two hundred years after that epoch the kings of Bactria, and of Ariana, or Afghânistan, were Greek in name and by race, and that the language of their coins and official documents was Greek; still such was the indifference, or such the difficulty of communication, that little or no intercourse was maintained by the people of the West with these Eastern colonies; and though using a common language, and derived from the same stock with the nation which boasted at the period its pre-eminence in intelligence and civilization, they are never referred to except as a *terra incognita*, that few knew and none cared about.

The whole of Western and Central Asia was, it is true, the scene of continuous strife and convulsion during the entire period of Greek ascendancy in these regions, and the events of most prominent interest in the world were occurring at the time in the West, which may account for some indifference towards the petty struggles for power amongst isolated chiefs and colonies in the far East. But the information left us of the acts and expeditions of western kings in this quarter, and even of Alexander himself, is exceedingly scanty and imperfect, and we seek in vain for any reason why it should be so. The reading public of the nineteenth century, who wade through volumes of controversy upon single events of local history, and who study accuracy, and the minutiæ of great men's proceedings and motives, with a mawkish and tedious interest, may well wonder to find so little curiosity displayed by the ancients, not only as to what was passing in Aria and Bactria, but even regarding the expeditions of Alexander, Seleucus, and Antiochus; and it is the more surprising that we have no consistent account in detail of the actions and enterprises of these kings, and especially of the first of them who so widely extended Greek dominion and Greek civilization, when such an example of correct and reasoning history had been set by Thucidydes, and when we know the pains taken by Alexander himself to cultivate the opinion of the learned of Greece, and to promote and encourage literature for the advancement of his own fame.

If, however, any man has a right to complain of the treatment he receives from history, and to lament the want of the *vatis sacri* to represent his actions and character in a true light to posterity, it is Alexander. The only justice done to him is in the affix of the title Great, which his name will carry with it to all time: we have little else regarding him but shallow superficial gossip, and libellous anecdotes, circulated with a view to detraction by the party which his genius and ascendancy excluded from power. It is from such materials that mankind is left to form its judgment upon the man, who holds amongst Greeks even a higher place than Julius Cæsar amongst Romans, and whose fame even Cæsar envied.

We do not refer here to the mere school impressions formed from Plutarch and others, of Alexander's rashness and violence, of his passion and drunkenness, his ambition for false glory, and his vain desire for deification, but to the means we possess of following this conqueror in the great enterprises he successfully carried through, and of marking the changes he effected or contemplated in the institutions and social condition of the world. There is nothing like a philosophical history, or even a true account in detail of Alexander's exploits and proceedings, in all the literature of Greece and Rome, for assuredly the works of Arrian and Quintus Curtius do not deserve that character.

In tracing, therefore, the history of the colonies which Alexander planted in the East, the first difficulty experienced arises from the very imperfect notices handed down to us, of the means by which he established those colonies, of their number and position, of the arrangements made for their internal government, and, what is of even more importance, of their relations with the natives of the regions in which they were placed.

It is well remarked by Professor Lassen, that Bactria and Aria, that is, the countries lying on either side of the Hindoo Koosh, between the Oxus and Indus rivers, are on the high road of Asiatic conquest, and have been the battle-field of every tribe and nation that has risen to dominion in the East. The history of this tract, therefore, if we had it complete and continuous, would tell more of the history of the world, and of the great revolutions in language, religion, civilization, and government, which have been brought about by conquest, and by the admixture of races resulting from conquest, than that of any other country on the face of the earth. For the want of this history, even for the period when Greek dominion and the Greek language gave means and facilities for preserving it, the modern learned are driven to speculation and conjecture, groping their way in dark uncertainty, and putting together facts gathered here and there at wide intervals, or drawing inferences from vague analogies of language, of feature, and of customs, whereon they build theories, which are overturned as fast as they are constructed.

It is now a little more than a century (1738) since Bayer wrote his treatise in Latin on the Greek colonies of Bactria, and proved to conviction, as the same Professor observes, the neglect these regions had experienced from writers of antiquity, by the meagreness of the details his industry and learning could discover in their works. He gave the names of not more than six kings of Greek origin, whom he found incidentally mentioned as having reigned in these countries, but the dates of their accessions and deaths, even the localities of the dominion of several, were left, and still remain, in uncertainty. It is only through coins since discovered, or by means of relics and inscriptions obtained in topes or tumuli, that we have made, or can hope to make, any advance in the knowledge of the past history of these regions beyond the point reached by Bayer, and the advance yet made is confined to a lengthened list of names, derived from coins, of kings before unheard of and unknown; but the coins, either by their execution, or by their type and emblems, or by the titles and superscriptions, afford circumstances from which to draw conclusions as to the connection of the kings with one another, or with known dynasties of the West. Moreover, the number and localities in which the coins are found, are circumstances from which to deduce arguments, as to the length of reigns and seats of government. Next to inscriptions, therefore, coins are the best evidence we can obtain, to support or supply the want of history. We have a few inscriptions, likewise, but they are in the new Arian language, and the decyphering of them remains to be accomplished.

It is not our purpose here to give in detail the history of the discoveries made in Bactrian numismatics. This has been well done by Professor Wilson in the publication prepared by him, and issued under the authority of the East India Company, for the purpose of giving to the world the results of Mr. Masson's researches, a work that does infinite honour to the patronage of that liberal and enlightened body. We will merely mention, that, until within the last ten years, the progress made in discovery was confined to occasional notices of stray coins with Greek names, which found their way to the cabinets of Europe, and were, by the learned, presumed to be Bactrian, because the coins were traced to that region, or to its vicinity, and were not ascribable to other known dynasties.

But since the mission to Kâbool and Bokhâra of the late Sir Alexander Burnes in 1831-32, there has been thrown quite a new light upon this branch of archæology, through the researches and discoveries of that officer, and of those engaged with him in that and subsequent missions, and especially through the impulse and direction given to the enquiries of others, who had even better opportunities than Burnes himself for prosecuting them. We refer in particular to the European officers in the service of Runjeet Singh, the ruler of the Punjab and Peshawur, amongst whom Generals Ventura, Alard and Court, are pre-eminent for the zeal with which they have applied themselves to such investigations. The great tope of Manykyâla was opened by General Ventura in April and May, 1830, when some coins and very curious relics were obtained. The example was followed some years after by General Court, who opened several other topes in the same vicinity. All these officers obtained rich rewards for their labours, and taking prompt means to make the results public, contributed greatly to advance the progress of discovery. But Dr. Hœnigberger, of the same service, was the first to draw the attention of Europe to the richness of the field for antiquities presented by Afghânistan;

for, returning in 1834 through Kâbool, Bulkh, Bokhâra, and Orenburgh, he brought with him a large collection of coins and relics made along that route, as well as in the Punjâb, and exhibited them in Germany, and afterwards in Paris, where they excited much curiosity, and were the subject of much learned speculation.

Nevertheless, it is to Mr. Masson, a private adventurer, who long resided at Kâbool, and enjoyed there the intimacy of the Nuwâb Jubâr Khan, and the powerful protection of his brother, Ameer Dost Mohummed, that we are indebted for the most complete and best directed local researches that have yet been made in these regions. Under the countenance, and with the aid of these brothers, Mr. Masson was able to employ himself for several years in seeking remains of the Greek dynasties, which had reigned in ancient times in the valley of the Kâbool river. He visited the supposed sites of various cities there, and identified the ruins, as well as the localities, as fit capitals for these extinct kingdoms; he opened likewise a great number of topes, or tumuli, at Daranta, near Julâlabad, and elsewhere in the same region, extracting from them relics of all kinds; and, thus having meployed six or eight years in collecting antiquities of the period of Greek and Scythian rule, (the coins he procured at Beghrâm, the presumed site of Alexandria *apud Caucasum*, are numbered by tens of thousands), he transmitted the whole to the

Museum of the India House, where they are now deposited, and lie open to the ready inspection of the curious and learned.

These investigations, be it observed, were prosecuted, and the results made known, some time before the British army advanced to Kâbool. We are indebted to that expedition for a great advance in our knowledge of the geography of the region of discovery; but in other departments of science, especially in numismatic and archæological researches, little further fruit was obtained. The harvest had already been gathered in, and the busy occupations of war and diplomacy afforded little leisure for the closer search required to glean the scattered remnant, and to pick up what had escaped those who had taken the lead in this field.

There may, however, be another reason, besides want of leisure, for the sudden arrestation of the progress of discovery, just at the period of British occupation of the country, in which it had made such rapid strides. In 1838, while the army was on its march to Afghânistan, the individual in India, who had done most to instigate enquiry, and to make public the results obtained, who brought to bear on each discovery a power of ingenious reasoning, acute comparison, and deep study, that made it tell as a step in advance, rewarding those who had contributed to bring it to light, and attracting new interest to the pursuit, was suddenly withdrawn from these favorite studies by an illness, which terminated in death. The journal of the Asiatic Society, established and conducted by Mr. James Prinsep at Calcutta, ceased after the year mentioned to be the inspiring organ to encourage and direct researches in this particular field. There wanted, when he was gone, the Promethean spark to kindle into light and life the dust and ashes dug out of these interesting ruins, and to extract language and sense from the rude characters, found traced on the venerable remains and relics obtained from them.

In the same year (1838) Europe lost Mons. Jacquet, a promising scholar of Paris, who, in the same field of Eastern archæological research, rivalled, and sometimes anticipated, the discoveries of James Prinsep in India. All, however, who have signalized themselves by successful study in this department are not gone. There is yet much to hope from the labours of Professors Lassen and Wilson, and we do not despair of finding some one of those who enjoyed the friendship and shared the studies of James Prinsep, who may yield to the desire of prosecuting these researches with Indian aids, and who may, perhaps, turn to equally good account the many facilities and advantages, there available.*

At present, having before us the various papers which appeared in the journal of the Asiatic Society, with Professor Wilson's exhibition of the results of

* We have reason to believe that Lieut. Cunningham, of the Bengal Engineers, is preparing a work on the antiquities of India and Afghanistan.

Mr. Masson's discoveries and researches; having, also, Professor Lassen's work on Bactrian and Indo-Scythian History, which was translated and published in the Indian journal, we take these as helping us to reach a landing place in this branch of discovery, beyond which it will require time, and a new series of efforts and researches to make further progress; and so regarding them, we shall endeavour to give such a summary of the results established as will make the general reader familiar with a subject, reserved hitherto for the learned antiquarian.

Professor Wilson has, in his publication of Mr. Masson's researches,* devoted a chapter to the collection of notices regarding Aria and Ariana from ancient writers, and in this work of labour and research he has effected all that the scholar can desire, and more than those, to whom we address ourselves, can need for preparation. He has, also, rightly judged, that for the proper comprehension of the subject it is indispensable to follow Alexander in his marches and encampments in these regions. We cannot, however, understand why, having carried Alexander through the country south of the Imaus, or Hindoo Koosh, to his cantonment of Alexandria at Beghrâm, near Kâbool, the Professor should

* Ariana Antiqua—a Descriptive Account of the Antiquities and Coins of Afghanistan, with a Memoir on the Buildings called Topes, by C. Masson, Esq., by H. H. Wilson, Esq., M.A., F.R.S. London, 1841.

altogether omit in this part of his work* the operations of two entire seasons in Bactria, north of that range, and proceed with Alexander's march to the Indus, as if these two campaigns had not intervened; for, in fact, it was in Bactria that the Greek power was most firmly established, and the march to the Punjâb would have been unsafe, if not impracticable, if that country had not been first reduced and colonized, so as to prevent Bessus and the Scythians from breaking in upon the line of communication with Media and Greece.

We shall also now briefly trace the march of Alexander, including these northern campaigns. The territory acquired by them, lying between the Hindoo Koosh and the Sir or Jaxartes, was much the richer and more important possession. It contained, according to Justin, a thousand populous cities, and was held by an army in the field of 15,000 men. Such was the force left by Alexander under Amyntas, to cover and support his colonies in Bactria, when he moved against India, and the condition of the tribes on the northern frontier required evidently the perpetual demonstration of readiness to repel and punish aggression, which only such an army could provide. When

* Professor Wilson does, in a different part of his work, viz., when treating of the geography of ancient Bactria, state the line of Alexander's march to the Jaxartes, but very briefly, and the continuity of the narrative of the expedition is lost by this division of the subject.

Bactria ultimately revolted from the Syrian kings, Aria and Afghânistan, or Ariana, followed with it, and the history of the one is so mixed up with the other, that the allotment of kings to either division at the time of separation, and the determination of the epochs of general sovereignty over both, are the main work by which the skill of the critic and antiquarian has to be tested. But it is not Bactria only that is closely linked with Ariana: we do not see how Parthia, and the rise and fall of Arsacidan power therein, can well be excluded from an enquiry into the history of these regions. For not only was the establishment of that dynasty contemporaneous with the revolt of Ariana and Bactria, and the relations between the three countries always intimate, but many of the Parthian kings extended their dominion over all three, and we find Parthian kings, and kings of kings, amongst those whose coins and relics are the materials, upon which we have to build the new fabric of history which is the result of recent discoveries.

To begin with the original conquest and colonization of these countries by the Greeks, Arrian tells us that Alexander the Great, after the pursuit and death of Darius, returned to the Caspian Sea, to complete the conquest of Hyrcania and of the Mardi. This was in June and July 330 B.C. The colonies here planted were the nucleus and main strength of the Parthian sovereignty, established eighty years afterwards by Arsaces. In August or September of the same year, Alexander marched into Aria and established a garrison, with a Persian Satrap, at Susia, its then capital. Professor Wilson finds on the map a place called Zuzan, on the desert side of the mountains west of Herât, and supposes that to be the Susia mentioned by Arrian. Dr. Thirlwall in his history identifies Susia with Toos, which is far within the Parthian frontier. We incline to the opinion that Subzâr or Subza-wâr, a city south of Herât, and within the region of fertility, is the Susia referred to, and certainly it is by situation a much more likely place for the capital indicated, than either of the other two. The garrison left here was overpowered as soon as Alexander had crossed the mountains in pursuit of Bessus, whereupon, returning hastily, he re-took the city, and capturing Artachaona* also, a place of refuge in the hills to the east of Susia, continued his operations southward to the Pontus, or Inland Sea, in which the Helmund terminates. Subzâr is in the direct line of such a march, which is another reason for preferring it for the capital of Aria. Alexander now effectually subjugated the entire country south of the Paropamisus, and placed Governors in Seestan and Arachotia, that is at Kandahar, or in Arghundāb, which Professor Wilson, with good reason, considers

* Mr. Elphinstone considers Artachaona to be Herât, but that could scarcely have been the stronghold of refuge, to which the revolting Persian would retire, being on the direct line of march to Bactria from Seestan. Sakhir, the capital of the Ghoris, is a much more likely position.

to be that region. He also placed a colony in a new city, built to control the Arians, which all authorities concur in regarding as the foundation of the afterwards, and still famous city of Herât. From this point, starting in the end of October, Alexander marched to the Kâbool valley, through a country occupied by Indians, and bordering on Arachotia, and his troops suffered exceedingly in the march from want, snow, and cold. We think the line of this march was the upper or hill route from Herât, running close under, and amongst the hills of the Paropamisan range, a region then occupied, according to all authorities, by an Indian race; and in confirmation of this line of march, we have the fact given by Arrian, that immediately on Alexander's return across the Hindoo Koosh from Bactria, his first act was to change the governor he had left in the Paropamisus, which shows that he had previously marched through and subjugated that hill country. Besides, the time (October) was short for a circuitous march, and if he had taken the route by Kandahar, and found snow in that vicinity, the passage by Ghuznee would have been quite closed, as we know by the sad experience of disasters in consequence.

The cantonment in which Alexander's army passed the winter of 330-29 B.C. was the Alexandria *apud Caucasum*,* the site of which has been

* Professor Wilson is inclined to the opinion that the ancient city, of which ruins are found at Beghrâm, was Nicæa, and that Alexandria was closer under the mountains in the Ghorbund

traced on the plain of Beghram near Chârikar, about thirty or forty miles north of Kabool. It is here that coins of the Greco-Bactrian kings and of their Scythian successors, have been found in much greater profusion than any where else, the place is likely, therefore, to have been the Capital of the region of the Kophen or Kâbool river.

Early in 329 B. C. Alexander crossed the Hindoo Koosh, and captured Drapsacus, or Indrâb. Thence, marching down the Oxus, he occupied and established garrisons in the country between that river and the mountains, while Bessus flying northward, across the Oxus, to Nautaka, or Karshi, was pursued and captured there by Ptolemy. Alexander then marched to Markanda, or Samarcand, and drove the Scythians before him to the Sir or Jaxartes, which river he crossed, and gained a great battle on the mountains opposite to Khojund. On the Jaxartes Alexander remained some time, establishing colonies for the defence of the passage of that river against Scythian incursion. While he was so occupied, Spitamenes came from the Kuzil Koom Desert and fell on Markanda in his rear. Though this partizan leader failed to capture the town of Markanda, he overpowered and cut to

valley. Beghrâm, however, is the more important position, commanding *all* the passes to Koondooz, and Khoolum east of the Kohi-Baba mountain, and seems much better adapted for a cantonment, and capital city, than a site in the close valley higher up. It appears, therefore, more likely to be the Alexandria referred to, which was the larger and more famous city of the two.

pieces a division of the Grecian army sent for its reinforcement; whereupon, Alexander counter-marching, took Kuropolis, which we suppose to be the ancient Kêsh, now Shuhur-Subz, and ravaged the entire valley of the Zurafshâr, the Polytimetus, or Samarkand river. As the year 329 B. C. was drawing to a close, when these operations were concluded, Alexander wintered his army at Ariaspe, or Zariâspe, which for many reasons we conclude to be Hazârasp ; First, because of its being in a military point of view the best position he could occupy in advance to check Spitamenes, being on the border of the desert, with the Oxus available to bring down his supplies. Secondly, because it is on the borders of Kharizm, and he was here in close communication with the Khorasmeni. Thirdly, because, while in this cantonment, he received a mission from the banks of the Wolga, for intercourse with which region it lies convenient, and lastly, from the great similarity of the name.

In the spring of 328 B. C., Alexander took the field in five divisions, to reduce the entire country between the Oxus and Jaxartes. Spitamenes was defeated, and slain at the beginning of the campaign, after a vain attempt to surprise Ariaspe, which confirms its identity with Hazârasp, a place well in advance, and, therefore, subject to such an attack. The rest of the season was devoted to the reduction of the numerous strongholds in the upper part of Soghdiana, and Mâwur-oon-nuhur, and to the establishment of colonies and garrisons to hold the country subdued. The winter of 328—27, B. C. was passed at Nautaka, or Karshi, and in the spring of 327, B. C. Alexander recrossed the Hindoo Koosh, and from Alexandria *apud Caucasum* commenced operations to reduce the country between that range and the Sofed-koh, that is in the Kohistân and Kâbool valley to the Indus. Alexander himself commanded to the north of the Kophen, or Kâbool river, and Hephœstion with Taxiles, the Indian king, took the route to the south. The latter arriving first at Attuk, built there the bridge of boats, by which Alexander's army passed into the Punjâb. Professors Lassen and Wilson follow these operations in considerable detail, adopting Arrian's report of them, which is confirmed by what we now know of the geography of the entire tract. For our present purpose, it is sufficient to state briefly that this entire country was subdued, and colonized like Bactria, in the months of April and May, 327 B. C. In July, 327 B. C. Porus was defeated on its banks of the Jihlum, and the months following were spent in colonizing and reducing the Punjâb, and in building a fleet for the descent of the Indus.

The greater part of 326 B. C. was passed in the passage down that river, and in operations to reduce the different races which occupied its banks. At the close of the rainy season, that is in about September or October, 326 B. C. Alexander commenced his return march in three divisions. The first, with the heavy baggage, he sent by Kandahar and Seestân, under Craterus. The second he led himself, by the sea coast, through Baloochistân and Makrân to Karmania (Kărmân). A third he sent by the then unexplored sea-route to the Persian Gulf, under Nearchus. All met at Suza towards the close of 325 B. C., the greatest hardships having been encountered by Alexander himself, in passing the arid deserts of southern Persia.

The result of these operations was, not merely that the conquering army swept over the face of Asia, leaving, like Tymoor, Chungeez Khan, and Attila, marks of ravage and desolation only in the regions traversed, but that the whole of the wide tract of country from the Mediterranean to the Indus, and from the Jaxartes and Caspian to the Sea, was subdued, garrisoned, and colonised,—made, in short, part of the Grecian empire, thus completely established in the East. We do not hear that any where the native population rebelled, and threw off the Grecian yoke, or overpowered the garrisons left to maintain possession of the country, excepting only in the Punjâb, near twenty years afterwards, during the troubles which followed the decease of Alexander. Everywhere else, the government and the armies were Greek; Hellenism was the system upon which the administration was organised and conducted, and society and religion yielded to the ascendancy of this dominant principle.

Alexander died in the spring of 323 B. C., that is, in the second year after his return to the ancient capitals of the Persian and Assyrian kings, leaving only a posthumous son. He caught a fever in the marshes of Mesopotamia, while planning a fresh capital for this vast empire in that central region. Consequently, we can only conjecture, what might have been the result, if his life had been spared to the ordinary average of human existence, or if an able successor had been left, to perfect the arrangements he had so auspiciously commenced, and to consolidate, secure, and completely Hellenise this wide dominion. But Alexander's empire, though of only ten years growth, was by no means transient. His colonies, and their institutions, manners, and language had struck deep root even in this short period, and we shall find that the impulse towards Hellenism had a lasting action in central Asia, the effects of which were felt for at least five hundred years after the decease of the conqueror. It is the especial object of these pages to endeavour to trace out this action in the regions where it had to maintain a struggle with barbarism, and to show how it finally sunk, and was extinguished, without exciting even a passing regret, or receiving the notice of a recording sentence, from any historian or writer of the distant West.

Alexander left, as above stated, no successor, for his brother Aridæus, and the posthumous child of Roshuna, or Roxana, called Alexander after his father, can scarcely be so considered. The consequence was, that the marshals, and men in power, became each independent, refusing obedience to their equals, or to any council of such at head-quarters.

The only system of government Alexander had had time to organize, was that of military occupation, and, of course, the military commandant of each district was the satrap, in whose person, and through whom, every authority of the state was locally exercised. While Alexander lived, the power of removal being absolute, and arbitrarily exerted, these satraps were effectually held in check; for none dared refuse a summons to the presence to answer a complaint, or to render account of any doubtful action; but on his death, the annihilation of this controling power, which existed but in the prestige of the conqueror's name and character, was immediate. There was no method of controlling, removing, or punishing a military satrap, but to direct against him the arms of a rival neighbour. In this manner Eumenes, the Governor of Cappadocia (B. C. 322), was employed against Craterus, whom he defeated and slew in action; and, being proscribed for this success by the Macedonians who loved Craterus, Antigonus (B. C. 320), was similarly employed against him. Eumenes was now worsted in turn, and driven out of Asia Minor (B. C. 318, 317); but jealousy of Antigonus led to his being re-employed against that chief, and the war between them was carried into Media and Parthia. Eumenes maintained the struggle for two years with eminent skill and good success, notwithstanding the ill-will of the Macedonians.

In the third campaign (B.C. 315), however, after a victory gained, he was delivered up prisoner to his rival by his own troops, and Antigonus becoming in consequence the sovereign of Asia, assumed openly the regal title. His first act after the overthrow of his rival was, to send the Argyraspides, Silvershields, a favored corps of *emeriti*, to be worn out by the hard duty of Arachotia, as a punishment for their bad faith to Eumenes. Seleucus (B. C. 314), Governor of Babylon, was soon after dispossessed by Antigonus, and fled to Ptolemy, whom he instigated to oppose Antigonus. The two invaded Syria and Phœnicia from Egypt (B.C. 312), and gaining some advantage, Seleucus started thence with 1000 men, and recovered Babylon, the population of which was friendly to him. Thence, influencing the garrisons of Media and Persia, he expelled the Governors for Antigonus, who was so occupied by his war with Ptolemy, that he could only send lieutenants against Seleucus, and these were successively defeated. In 305 B.C., Seleucus gaining a great victory over Nicanor, one of these lieutenants, followed it up by seizing and adding to his own government, the whole of Media, Hyrcania, Parthia, Bactria, and Aria, and all the countries as far as the Indus. In 303, he crossed that river to make war on Chundra Goopta (Sandracottus), who, during these contentions, had expelled the Grecian garrisons from the Punjâb, and had so recovered that country for the native sovereigns of India. Seleucus made, however, a hasty peace with Chundra Goopta, ceding the Punjâb as far as the Indus,* and receiving 500 elephants, being called back suddenly for a final struggle with Antigonus. In this war with that chief, Lysimachus assisted from Thrace, as well as Ptolemy from Egypt, and Antigonus being driven into Phrygia, was there defeated and slain by Seleucus in 301 B.C.

From this period till 280 B.C., when Seleucus Nicator was assassinated by Ptolemy Ceraunus, after a victory gained over Lysimachus, in which that king also was slain, the whole of Asia to the Indus and Jaxartes, was under the Syrian king. The son of Seleucus, Antiochus Soter, from 280 to 261 B.C., reigned also undisturbed over the same territory, and left it to his son, Antiochus Theus. This last king, however, getting involved in a difficult war with Ptolemy Philadelphus, and his successor, Euergetes, neglected his Eastern possessions. Bactria, in consequence, declared its independence under Theodotus, or Diodotus, in 256, or 255 B.C. according to Bayer. Parthia followed about the year† 250 B.C., the revolt of this province being ascribed to an attempt of Agathocles, the local Governor, upon the person of a noble youth named Tiridates, which his brother, Arsaces, resented by conspiring

* Strabo says Arachotia was also ceded, but this seems doubtful. Kuchchee to the Bolan Pass, with the Valley of the Indus, may be the region intended.

† Vaillant gives the year 256 B.C. for the date of Arsaces' revolt in Parthia, basing the date on the consuls, named by Justin as in office for the year. The year 250 B.C. seems, however, preferably established.

and slaying the Governor. To secure himself, he seized the government, and the revolt being neglected, he continued to strengthen himself, until in 241 B.C., he was able to add Hyrcania to his original government of Parthia, which lay between Herât and the Caspian, and is now the province of which Mushud is the capital.*

The native country of Arsaces is uncertain. By some he is called a Dahian, that is, a native of Soghd. By others, a Bactrian. Moses of Chorene, the historian of Armenia, who lived in the fifth century of our era, when the Arsacidan dynasties had recently been expelled from both Parthia and Armenia, declares the first Arsaces to have been a native of Bulkh. He adds, that the dynasty were called Balhavenses, or Pahlaveean, from the circumstance that Bulkh was added to Parthia, and made its seat of Government, by the son of Arsaces, meaning Mithridates, the great-grandson. Strabo says that Arsaces was a Bactrian, who had fled to Parthia, because the rival party of Theodotus had prevailed in his native city, which is not at all inconsistent with the Armenian's story. We give in a note below the words of Moses from the Latin translation,† because the passages are curious, and contain the earliest mention we find anywhere of

* The Persians consider Khorasan to include Herât and the Paropamisus, and northward to extend as far as Merv, otherwise Parthia might be described by that name.

† Itaque, ut diximus, post sexaginta annos, quam Alexander mortuus est,‖ Parthis imperitavit Arsaces, fortis in urbe orientis quæ vocatur *Balcha* in regione Cusæorum. (Qy. Hindoo

the city of Bulkh, by that name, showing that it could not well be identical with Ariaspe, as is by some supposed.

Whatever may have been the country and race to which Arsaces belonged, we find him using Greek only on his coins, and in his public letters and correspondence. There is no other language or character found on any coin of known Parthian mintage and type. Some coins indeed, with Parthian names and bilingual superscriptions, and one of an Arsaces, have recently been discovered in Afghanistân, and on them we find the Parthian title of king of kings: still, it is doubtful whether these are the coins of Parthian kings of kings, or of Satraps, who declared their independence, and assumed that lofty title; and, even if some of them be coins of real sovereigns of Parthia, they will have been minted locally, to provide a local currency for Afghanistân.

The Arsacidan coins of Parthia proper, have ordinarily the sovereign's head, without any in-

Koosh) posita.—Book II., cap. II. p. 54.—again in page 188, De regiis stupibus. "Tum filius ejus, Arsaces, qui cognominatus est magnus, qui Antiochum occidit, Volarsacem fratrem suum Armeniæ regem fecit, et ab se secundum constituit. Ipse autem, *Balham* profectus, regnum suum ibi fundavit: ac propterea progenies ejus Balhavenses nominatur, sicut Volarsacis fratris sui proles, ab progenitore, Arsacidum nomen invenit; illi autem sunt reges Balhavenses.

N.B. The Arsaces here referred to, who set up his brother in Armenia, and established his own sovereignty in Bulkh was Mithridates Ist.

scription on one side; on the other, a sitting figure with a bow held out, and the inscription in Greek on four sides, forming a square on the face of the coin.* This inscription has seldom any but the family name of Arsaces, with the title ΒΑΣΙΛΕΥΣ or ΒΑΣΙΛΕΥΣ ΒΑΣΙΛΕΩΝ, and various epithets, ΜΕΓΑΣ, ΔΙΚΑΙΟΣ, ΕΠΙΦΑΝΗΣ, ΕΥΕΡΓΕΤΗΣ, ΖΗΝΙΟΣ, or ΞΕΙΝΙΟΣ, ΘΕΟΣ, ΝΙΚΑΤΩΡ, ΦΙΛΕΛΛΗΝΟΣ, ΘΕΟΠΑΤΗΡ, &c. all pure Greek, and generally in the genitive case. Only one of the Bilingual coins of Afghanistan yet found, has the family name of Arsaces on it, and all these coins, as we shall show hereafter, differ in other respects from those of known Arsacidan type. It is not easy to classify, and assign the Arsacidan coins to the known sovereigns of Parthia, for the name Arsaces is, as above stated, common to all, and history does not tell us which of the race took the particular epithets and titles we find on them. But we have this criterion, that Basileus only, or with such epithets as just, illustrious, and other modest titles of that kind, will indicate the earliest of the race. Great king of kings was the title first assumed

* Some of Vonones have his name on the obverse, in imitation probably of the Romans, amongst whom he was educated: one of these is given by Professor Wilson, for comparison with the Afghan coins of the same name. It has on the reverse a Victory, instead of the sitting figure with a bow: and several of the later Arsacidan kings coined also with a winged Victory presenting a crown, on the reverse, which is a device we find on the Ario-Parthian coins. The obverse, however, of these latter is widely different.

by Mithridates II., which Asiatic form must have been adopted after the conquest and acquisition of countries bordering on India, for we find the same title on coins of Scythian kings, who acquired dominion in those regions at the same period, and we have reason to believe it to be of Indian origin.

There is at the India House a very complete cabinet of Arsacidan coins, which was presented to the East India Company by Sir H. Willock, now deputy chairman. We doubt if any other Museum has one so full. It will be seen upon examination of the coins, that the earliest have on the obverse the helmeted head of a young man with no inscription at all; on the reverse, is the sitting figure above described, with a bow, and the simple legend, ΑΡΣΑΚΟΥ ΒΑΣΙΛΕΩΣ. This coin we cannot hesitate to assign to the first Arsaces. Next, we have the same helmeted head, with an inscription on the reverse, bearing the same sitting figure, ΑΡΣΑΚΟΥ ΒΑΣΙΛΕΩΣ ΜΕΓΑΛΟΥ, which may be of the same king, after his defeat and capture of Seleucus, an exploit entitling him to the epithet. Then we have the same inscription, and reverse, with a filleted head on the obverse, having the hair full over the shoulders, as is usual with kings of this race. Next, we have a similar filleted head, with a similar reverse, and the inscription ΑΡΣΑΚΟΥ ΒΑΣΙΛΕΩΣ ΕΠΙΦΑΝΟΥΣ. A fifth variety has, with a nearly similar obverse and reverse, the inscription ΑΡΣΑΚΟΥ ΦΙΛΟΠΑΤΡΟΣ ΒΑΣΙΛΕΩΣ ΜΕΓΑΛΟΥ, which word, Philopater is considered by numismatists to denote association with the father while living; but history is silent as to which of the early Arsacides falls within this category. A sixth variety has, on a similar coin in other respects, the inscription, ΑΡΣΑΚΟΥ ΘΕΟΠΡΟΠΟΥ ΒΑΣΙΛΕΩΣ ΜΕΓΑΛΟΥ. If we assign these six varieties to the predecessors of Mithridates II.*, he will be the first crowned king of kings of this race; and, as his reign was one of Arsacidan greatest power and pride, the evidence of coins supports and confirms that of history. The early coins we have noticed are not mentioned by Vaillant, but Mionnet in his great work has supplied the omission, and corrected Vaillant's very arbitrary and capricious allotment of coins to kings of this race; Visconti and several other foreign numismatists have also devoted themselves to this subject, so that there is little new or original to be added at this day. Nevertheless, Professor Wilson would have made his work on Arianian relics more complete, by including the series of Arsacidan coins contained in the cabinet referred to. Perhaps, however, the description of them, as of the Sassanian series in the same Museum, is reserved for the special catalogue of the library and curiosities, which is now under preparation.

We cannot take leave of this cabinet without

* Mithridates I. is by some supposed to have called himself King of Kings; but the date of the reign of the second of the name is more consistent with the period when this title was assumed in Bactria. Eucratides, the cotemporary of Mithridates I., only called himself Great King.

noticing especially two coins it contains of Arsacidan kings, which are historical, and very peculiar. One bears the usual filleted head, with full locks, and no inscription on the obverse; but on the reverse has a female bust, with prominent Roman features, and the superscription ΘΕΡΜΟΥΣΑΣ, ΒΑΣΙΛΙΣΣΑΣ ΘΕΑΣ ΟΥΡΑΝΙΑΣ. This, of course, is a coin of Phrahates, who married Thermusa, the maid *(Ancilla)* presented to him by Anthony, and who yielded to this queen's influence so far, as to send his four other sons as hostages to Augustus, in order to make way for the succession of her son, Phrahataces, by whom he was soon after poisoned.

The other peculiar coin is of Vonones, of which there are three specimens. A drawing of it is given by Professor Wilson in Plate XV. of his Ariana, for comparison with the coins of Vonones, found in Afghânistan. On one side is the head of Vonones, with the simple inscription ΒΑΣΙΛΕΥΣ ΟΝΩΝΗϹ in the nominative case, according to Roman taste. On the reverse is a Victory, with the inscription ΒΑΣΙΛΕΥϹ ΟΝΩΝΗϹ ΝΕΙΚΗϹΑϹ ΑΡΤΑΒΑΝΟΝ, thus identifying him as the son of Phrahates, invited from Rome, and successful at first against Artabanus, but expelled soon after. The absence of any other coinage of this king confirms what Tacitus reports of his short lived power, as the inscription does the manner of his accession.

Having premised this, we will now shortly give the dynasty of Arsacidan kings, with a notice of such circumstances as are to be gathered from Greek and Roman authors, in respect to each. We have nowhere a consecutive history of the race or country, written with authority from native records, or at a period when events were recent, and the succession of sovereigns easily traced and ascertained; but, of course, the notices of Parthia, in the classic authors of Greece and Rome, are more frequent than those of Bactria, Aria, and countries farther East, because Parthian kings came more frequently into collision with the sovereigns and nations of Europe, and of Western Asia.

B.C. 254-250. ARSACES I., a native of Bulkh in Bactria, revolted from Antiochus Theus, slaying Agathocles, the Governor of Parthia. In 241 B.C. he seized Hyrcania, and fearing invasion, prepared against a combined attack from Syria and Bactria; but Theodotus of Bactria dying, he entered into a strict alliance with the second Theodotus, and so awaited the attack from Syria. In 236 B.C. Seleucus Kallinicus having made peace with Egypt, made a first expedition against Parthia, which was of little effect. In 230 B.C. he made a second expedition, in which he at first drove Arsaces into Khârizm, but was afterwards defeated and made prisoner by this king, who thereupon took the title of Megas Basileus. Arsaces is said to have been killed in action with Ariarathes of Cappadocia, but the date and circumstances are not known.* Seleucus died by a fall from his horse while returning from his captivity.

About B.C. 220. II. ARSACES II. ARTABANUS,† son of the last king, continued to extend and strengthen the Parthian empire, adding Media while Antiochus Magnus was at war with Egypt. In 212, Antiochus commenced operations against Arsaces, and recovered Media. Soon after, he drove Arsaces out of Parthia, leaving him only Hyrcania. In 210, Antiochus captured Syringis, a city of that country; but Arsaces calling in the Scythians, again made

* Vaillant quoting Arrian, *apud Syncellum*, supposes Arsaces to have been killed in the second year after declaring his independence, and to have been succeeded by his brother, Tiridates. But we find nothing of this in Justin or Strabo, and Arsaces' name would not have been carried down, if his life and power had been so little enduring. The accession of Tiridates, the brother, seems therefore very doubtful. Syncellus was a Byzantine, who lived in the time of Charlemagne. He cites Arrian, in his Chronology, for the fact, that it was Agathocles, and not Pherecles, who committed the outrage which led to the insurrection; and although it may thence be inferred, that Arrian's Parthian History was then extant, Syncellus does not take any other facts from it, nor refer to it in support of his assignment of only two years for the reign of the first Arsaces, in opposition to Justin and Strabo. It is probable that one of the brothers died after two years, but not Arsaces.

† Vaillant gives the year 217 B.C. for that of the accession of Artabanus, allowing two years to the first Arsaces, and thirty-seven to Tiridates, and following in this the Chronological tables of Syncellus.

head with an army of 100,000 men, and in 208 B.C. Antiochus made peace with him, ceding Parthia and Hyrcania in consideration of aid in the war against Bactria and Aria. Polybius calls the king opposed to Antiochus, Artabanus, but other authorities describe him only as the second Arsaces, son of the founder of the dynasty. The date of his decease is not indicated with any certainty.

B.C. 196. III. ARSACES PRIAPATIUS, or PHRIADATIUS, son of the last king. We know of no occurrences of this reign, except that it lasted fifteen years, was peaceable, and of good repute, and that the king left three sons, all of whom reigned; viz., Phrahates, Mithridates, and Artabanes.

B.C. 181. IV. ARSACES PHRAHATES I. The Mardi were reduced in this reign, but it was short and inglorious.

B.C. 177. V. ARSACES MITHRIDATES I. The date of accession is uncertain. Some placing it as early as 180 B.C., and others as late as 165 B.C. It is of this king that Moses of Chorene writes, that he set up his brother in Armenia, and removed the seat of his own government to Bulkh, which he had subdued; all Media and Persia, also, submitted to him at one time, and he captured Babylon. In 140 B.C. Demetrius Nicator attacked Parthia, and being joined by many of the Greek colonists recently subjugated by Mithridates, gained some successes, but in a second campaign was made prisoner by treachery, according to Justin *(simulatione pacis)*. He was well treated, and married to a daughter of the Parthian king, but did not recover his liberty until released by Phrahates, when Parthia was attacked again ten years after by his brother. After the defeat of Demetrius, Mithridates made a successful expedition into India. He had previously brought under his dominion the greater part of what had formed the empire of his cotemporary, Eucratides; that is, besides Western Bactria, Aria, Seestan, and Arachotia; but Soghdiana was seized by the Scythians.

B. C. 139. VI. ARSACES PHRAHATES II., son of Mithridates, succeeded his father soon after the expedition into India, but the exact date is nowhere stated. In 131 B.C. Antiochus Sidetes made war on Parthia with much success at first, from the same cause that had favored Demetrius; that is, the favor of the Greco-Bactrians, who were disaffected towards Parthia; but in 130 B.C. he was defeated in a great battle and slain. Phrahates had called in the Scythians to aid in this war; after its close, they committed ravages, to punish which, Phrahates took the field against them, and was slain in action. There is reason to believe that Bactria was in this reign subjugated entirely by Scythians.

B.C. 126. VII. ARSACES ARTABANES, uncle of Phrahates, and youngest son of Priapatius, succeeded, but he too was wounded in an action with the Tochari Scythians, and died of the wound.

B.C. 115. VIII. ARSACES MITHRIDATES II., called also *Great*, son of Artabanes, succeeded. He gained advantages, and made some settlement with the Scythians, and by their aid is supposed to have been established as nominal sovereign over Western Bactria, Aria, and at one time as far as the Indus in Southern Afghanistan. The Scythians, however, are in this reign supposed, under Azes and his successors, to have held dominion in Bulkh and Kabool, and thence to have conquered the Punjab. The Tochari, Yeutchi, or White Huns, were settled under Asian kings in Sogdiana, and the mountainous country north of the Oxus. In the time of this king a letter was addressed to Rome, and ambassadors came from Mithridates to Sylla, the Dictator. He died about 85 B.C. *gloriosâ senectute*, but the date is uncertain.

B.C. 85. A period of contention and civil war followed, and if the *kings of kings* of Parthian race, whose coins are found in Afghanistan, of pure Greek type, were a separate dynasty, this will be the period when most probably their independence was declared.

XI. MNASKIRES and X. PHRAHATES, are mentioned as rivals for the throne of Parthia, but little is known of either. The Scythians increased in power during these troubles, and in 77 B.C. placed a king on the Parthian throne.

B. C. 77. XI. ARSACES SINATRUX, or SANATROIKES, as written on his coins. The Sakarauli Scythians placed this king on the throne. A letter to him from Mithridates of Pontus is preserved in Sallust's fragments, but it can scarcely be genuine, and seems to be of Roman fabrication. His reign was marked by no event of note.

B. C. 67. XII. ARSACES PHRAHATES III. son of Sinatrux, succeeded his father, and soon after entered into treaty with Pompey, during the war of Rome with Tigranes of Armenia. He reigned peaceably for ten years. In 56 B. C. his two sons, Orodes and Mithridates, conspired and slew him: then quarrelling for the succession, Orodes prevailed, and Mithridates sought refuge and succour from Gabinius, Pompey's lieutenant, in Syria. But he being called into Egypt, Mithridates attempted alone to displace his brother, but was captured and put to death.

B. C. 55. XIII. ARSACES ORODES reigned when Crassus made his disastrous expedition, and was defeated, and slain by Surenas. He also was opposed to Ventidius, the lieutenant of Anthony: and his favorite son and heir apparent Pakores was defeated and slain by that general in B. C. 39. Orodes much grieved at the loss, nominated another son named Phrahates to be his heir, and was by him circumvented and slain.

B. C. 37. XIV. ARSACES PHRAHATES. A party attempted to exclude this son for the parricide, but with Scythian aid he established himself, and was on the throne when Anthony invaded Parthia, and penetrating 300 miles beyond the Armenian frontier (the Kur river), laid seige to Praaspa.* Failing in the seige, Anthony made a disastrous retreat. A brother and rival of Phrahates, named Tiridates, sought refuge and succour from Augustus Cæsar after Anthony's death; and Augustus using the opportunity, obtained from Phrahates restoration of the standards taken from Crassus, with four sons of the king to reside at Rome for education and as hostages. A fifth son, Phrahataces, by the Italian queen, Thermusa, whose influence had sent away the hostages, conspired against his father, and got rid of him by poison, in the year 4 A. D. but he was not allowed to reign.

A. D. 4. XV. ARSACES ORODES II. Convulsions followed the death of Phrahates, and Orodes, a son, was set up, whose civil war with his

* Seleucia, on the Tigris, was the Capital in this reign, but when it became so is uncertain. Anthony declared he would treat when he arrived there, upon which the Parthian Ambassador, said "Sooner will hair grow on the palms of these hands than you take Seleucia."

parricide brother lasted nearly ten years. Orodes was himself put to death for his cruelty, about 14 A.D., and a son of Phrahates, was asked from Rome.

A. D. 14. XVI. ARSACES VONONES the First,* was sent by Tiberius Cæsar on the application of a party at the capital of Parthia, and gaining a victory over Artabanus, was established as king in Seleucia. But becoming unpopular from his un-Asiatic habits, Artabanus returned and expelled him again, whereupon he retired to Armenia, but being expelled thence also, died in Syria.

A. D. 18. XVII. ARSACES ARTABANUS of Media, said by Tacitus to be descended, on the mother's side only, from Arsaces, and to have been educated amongst the *Dahæ* Scythians, was set up by them, and though unpopular for his cruelty, maintained himself by the same means. In A. D. 35, Tiberius sent from Rome a second son of Phrahates, called by that name, and Artabanus was expelled again from Seleucia, and lived for a time in great extremity, in the wilds of Hyrcania, but returned and again drove out his rival. He died, leaving, accord-

* Vaillant in his Chronological Canon at the end of Vol. I. says, Vonones was invited in A. D. 6, but in the annals at the commencement, A. D. 14 is the date, and this seems preferable, and more consistent with both Tacitus and Josephus. Professor Wilson has given a reign of twenty-four years to this king, through the mistake of placing its commencement in 6 B. C., instead of 6 A. D., which latter date even is not warranted by authority.

ing to Josephus, seven sons, Darius, Bardanes, Gotarzes, Orodes, Volageses, Pakores, and Tiridates. Of these, according to the same author, he nominated Bardanes his successor, but according to Tacitus, he was slain by his brother Gotarzes, who seized and held the throne, until conquered by Bardanes.

A. D. 41. XVIII. ARSACES BARDANES. This king was in alliance with Rome. According to Josephus, his brothers yielded the sovereignty to him, but other authorities state that he overpowered them after a civil war.* His reign was glorious, though short. According to Tacitus, he extended his dominion as far as

* It is quite impossible to reconcile the account given by Josephus with the short but seemingly authoritative notice of these two kings, found in Tacitus; Josephus mentions them in connection with Izates of Adiabene, who embraced Judiasm, and was circumcised, and says that Artabanus, when expelled the second time from Seleucia, took refuge with Izates, and was by him restored: that dying soon after, he left the throne to Bardanes, whose name he writes Ουαρδάνης, and that this king sought a confederacy with Izates against Rome, which he disapproving, was threatened in consequence with invasion. But the Parthians not disposed to a war with Rome, made away with Bardanes, and set up his brother Gotarzes, who also dying soon after, Vologeses, another brother, succeeded, and he assigned Media to his brother Pakores, and Armenia to another brother, Tiridates. All this is irreconcileable with the reported glories of Bardanes, in whose court Philostratus places Apollonius Tyaneus as a guest for some years, and makes him journey with his safeguard through Bactria to India; and as this account of the impostor was written in the reign of Severus, it shows the received notions of the day respecting Bardanes.

the river Sinde? the boundary of the country of the Dahæ, which we conclude to be to the Indus south, and north east as far as Soghdiana, then in the possession of the Yeutchi Scythians, who had overpowered the Dahæ. He was cut off by treachery while hunting.

A. D. 47. XIX. ARSACES GOTARZES (Persian Godurz), the next brother then succeeded. He is declared by Tacitus to have been a worshipper of Hercules, supported by Scythian auxiliaries. Claudius, the emperor, gave his countenance and active support to Mihardates, a son of Vonones, the hostage king, but he failed in an attempt on the throne of Parthia, and Gotarzes died shortly after a natural death.

A.D. 49. XX. ARSACES VONONES II. This reign also was short and inglorious. The coins ONΩNOϒ, found in Afghanistan, with the title of king of kings in the Arian characters and language, as well as in Greek, are supposed by some to be of this king, but there is nothing known of his reign or character to confirm the supposition. He lost his throne and life in a contest with Vologeses.

A. D. 52. XXI. ARSACES VOLOGESES, son of Gotarzes, by a Greek public woman (*pellex*), according to Tacitus, succeeded. This king warred with Rome for Armenia, and driving out two legions, established his brother Tiridates there. He had a Scythian war also on his hands in Hyrcania, and is supposed by Professor Lassen to have recovered Kabool and Kandahar from the Kadphises race of kings, being identified by the Professor with the Abagasus, whose coins are found in the Kabool valley, but this seems very doubtful. Vologeses is the king who addressed Vespasian assuming the title of king of kings, which was returned by that Emperor with his own name only, "Vespasian to Arsaces king of kings." The reign was happy and glorious, and of some length.

A.D. 85. XXII. ARSACES ARTABANUS III. son of Vologeses succeeded, but we know little of him or of his reign.

A.D. 99. XXII. ARSACES PAKORES. This reign also was long, but marked by no event of note. Pakores is declared to have been the friend of Rome, and ally of Decebalus, king of the Daci. The coin found of Pakores, with an Arian legend, may be of this king, and would show a wide dominion in the East, but more probably it is the coin of a Satrap who assumed royalty.

A.D. 115. XXIV. ARSACES KHOSROES (Persian Khosroo), brother of Pakores succeeded, and was the cotemporary of Trajan. He defeated that Emperor's lieutenant Maximus in Mesopotamia, whereupon Trajan, fitting out a large army, and building boats on the Euphrates, conquered the entire valley of that river, and of the Tigris also to the sea, and set up in Seleucia on the Tigris, another Parthian king, called by Roman authors Parthanaspatis. On Trajan's death, Khosroes recovered Mesopotamia, and Adrian granted a peace ceding all the country east of the Euphrates. This reign also was long.

A.D. 160. XXV. ARSACES VOLOGESES, the eldest son of Khosroes succeeded. He made peace and an alliance with the Alani, and cut off the Roman legions stationed in Armenia. But the Roman generals, Priscus and Cassius retrieved affairs in that province, and carrying the war into Persia, captured Babylon and Seleucia, in the time of Verus and Antoninus. The last-named granted a peace after the death of Verus.

A.D. 195. XXVI. ARSACES VOLOGESES III., son of Sinatrux, brother of the last king succeeded. This was the king opposed to Severus when he invaded Mesopotamia, and took Ctesiphon. He was afterwards involved in a civil war with Artabanus, during which he died a natural death.

A. D. 215. XXVII. ARSACES ARTABANUS becoming sole king, was involved in a war with Rome; and Caracalla, soliciting his daughter in marriage, plotted to take him prisoner, or to cut him off at a conference. Many Parthian nobles were sacrificed, but Artabanus escaping, commenced a war of revenge, in which he made great ravage, and being opposed by Macrinus, a drawn battle of an entire day was fought, with great slaughter on both sides. Artabanus preparing to recommence the battle next day, was informed of the death of his enemy Caracalla, and obtained from Macrinus some concessions which put an end to the war. Ardeshur Babakan, or Artaxerxes, was a distinguished officer of the Parthian army, and an object of jealousy in consequence. He was slighted, and revolted, and after three severe battles, conquered and slew Artabanus, subverting the Arsacidan dynasty, and establishing his own, that of the Sessanians in 235 B.C.; his last victory was gained at Bulkh, and he was there crowned, according to Persian authority.

Thus closed the Greco-Parthian dominion in Central Asia, after a continuance of very nearly 500 years. The capital in the time of the Cæsars was at Seleucia on the Tigris, and the removal from the original territory of Mushud and Toos was most probably compulsory, in consequence of the growing power and encroachments of the Scythians. It must at any rate have weakened the hold of this race of kings upon their eastern provinces. The system of government was purely Asiatic; that is, by subordinate satraps, or sovereigns, each possessing full and absolute authority over the persons and properties of all the subjects of the state. Bearing this in mind, we have the less reason to wonder at finding Parthians asserting independence and coining with arrogant titles in Afghanistan; of this, however, more hereafter.

We have deemed it necessary to premise this brief summary of the history of Parthia, during its transition back from Hellenism to a purely Asiatic sovereignty, and condition of society, because without continual reference to its position and relations with the countries bordering on it, the condition of Bactria, Aria, and of Kabool, *i. e.*, the country of the Kophenes river, would scarcely be intelligible.

We shall now put together what the learning and research of western scholars have extracted from ancient authors, and from modern discoveries, in respect to those more distant regions; and here we have to remark, that amongst cotemporary writers on this subject, Professor Lassen* only has endeavoured to generalize the data, and to classify the kings, whose names have come to light, systematically by dynasties. Others have been content to treat the subject more strictly numismatically, and to discuss the coins rather than the historical probabilities connected with the names they bear, and Professor Wilson, especially, has preferred that course. There is undoubtedly in Professor Lassen's method something very national and German; he launches boldly into the wide ocean of conjecture to supply deficiencies in his information, and builds theories regarding his dynasties, nations, and races,

* Zur Geschichte der Grechischen Konige in Bactrien, by Christian Lassen. Boun, 1838. (Translated in Calcutta, 1840.)

without any very substantial stratum of authoritative facts for a foundation, and with materials quarried often in the imagination. The course of our English professor is the safer for the critic, and may on that account have more lasting value. He has ordinarily the support of Mionnet, Visconti, P. Rochette, and other eminent numismatists, for the inferences he draws, and assigns dates to the different kings, of whom no mention is made in history, upon evidence afforded by the coins in their execution, or through some similarity of emblems and symbols with those of other countries, or with one another.

We confess, however, that we incline to adopt many of Professor Lassen's speculations, theoretical as they are, and think the plan of systematic arrangement which he has adopted far preferable for the general reader. We shall proceed, therefore, to explain the principles of his classification, noticing the principal differences of opinion between him and Professor Wilson, and adding, with the information brought to light since the works of both Professors were written, a theory of our own, in respect to one of the Scythian dynasties, resuscitated by these discoveries.

Professor Lassen, using as landmarks those kings, whose names he finds mentioned in ancient authors with any circumstances to connect them with particular regions, or with settled dates and known events, arranges the new kings, whose coins have been recently discovered, on the following principles, which, whether original or borrowed from preceding antiquarians, are at least rational, and command assent.

First, one or two coins only have yet been found of Theodotus, but these, as well as the coins of Euthydemus, and of Demetrius, the known earliest kings of Bactria and Ariana, resemble the coins of the Seleucidæ, or Greco-Syrian kings; they are of excellent workmanship, with fine heads on the obverse, and some mythological emblem on the reverse, and with superscriptions generally confined to the latter side, in the Greek language only. Such being the character of the earliest coins, any similar that have been, or may be found, with new Greek names and simple titles can, it is assumed, belong only to the same race and period. Coins of Heliocles, Antimachus, Agathocles, and Eucratides, have been discovered, answering precisely to this description; but there is this difference, that of all these kings, there are also coins with bilingual inscriptions, whereas, of the earliest kings, there are none yet found that are not purely and exclusively Greek. These kings, therefore, or some of them, the two last named supposed the earliest, taking up the coinage from their predecessors, in the provinces which used Greek only, may fairly be presumed to have made the change during their reigns, by introducing the new language, also, where it was vernacular, which must have been in some part of their dominions. Their reigns, too, must, it is assumed, have preceded those of kings, of whom none but bilingual coins exist, unless the latter held dominion in different territories. The new language we find called Arian, Arianian, Bactrian, and Kaboolian (we prefer the first of these names), according to the supposed locality of its native use. All the kings who adopted it for their coins place it only on the reverse, reserving the original Greek for the obverse, with the head or bust. Eucratides is a known king, cotemporary with Mithridates I. of Parthia; the others above named are new: of them more hereafter.

Secondly. There are coins with Greek inscriptions only, of inferior workmanship, and with Barbarian names; some of these have pure Greek titles, as ΣΩΤΗΡ, ΜΕΓΑΣ, ΔΙΚΑΙΟΣ, &c., and some have both barbarian names and titles. All these Professor Lassen ascribes to Scythian dynasties, who are known to have overrun Soghdiana and Bactria in the second century before our era, and subsequently to have established themselves in Afghanistan. The coins of this description of different types he assigns to different races and periods of this Scythian dominion, and, in doing so, is compelled to deal largely with theory and conjecture, seeking supports from Chinese and Mongolian sources, as well as from classic authors.

Thirdly. By far the largest number of the new coins found are bilingual, of excellent workmanship. Many have fine Greek heads, with plain inscriptions on one side, and on the other some type from Grecian mythology, as Jupiter, Minerva, Hercules, or the Dioscuri (Castor and Pollux). Some have a horseman on the obverse, or a Victory with wings, or an elephant, or a Bactrian camel, and some have on the reverse a device of this description, and some on both sides; but the kings' names are in pure Greek, the inscriptions plain, and the strange language on the reverse having been decyphered, by using the names as a key to the alphabet, proves to be Sanscrit, or Pracrit, the vernacular form of Sanscrit, written semitically from right to left. These bilingual coins, like the pure Greek coins, are of several races of kings: Of some both names and titles are pure Greek, with Arian words, exactly corresponding; of some, the names are Parthian, and titles Greek, with Arian inscriptions, not exactly corresponding; of others, again, the names are barbarian, but titles Greek, and exactly translated into Arian. But there is a fourth class, with barbarian names and titles in scarcely legible Greek characters, and with Arian inscriptions, not corresponding, and not decypherable, or rather not yet decyphered. All these belong, of course, to different races and dynasties, and the perspicacity of the critic is shown in the arrangement and classification of the names by these criteria.

Fourthly. There is again another class of coins of copper, and roughly executed, with Greek inscriptions and names on one side, and on the other the kings' name, only without any title, in ancient Sanscrit characters, exactly corresponding with those of Asoka's inscriptions on the rocks of Girnar and Cuttack, and on the pillars of Dehli, Bhitari, and Allahabad. Only two kings, Agathocles and Pantaleon, are yet known to have coined money with such inscriptions, and the former coined also with Greek inscriptions only.

Professor Lassen argues, with great apparent reason, that, as we find pure Greek to be carried on through Scythian dynasties, and the first use of Arian inscriptions to be by Greeks, and not by Scythians, the new language is not of Scythian origin: and further, that it was not in use in the regions of this particular Greco-Scythian coinage; that is, in Bactria and Soghdiana, the known Greek kings of which, Theodotus, Euthydemus, &c., coined only Greek, like these Scythians. Further, because the language, so far as it has yet been decyphered, proves to be Sanscrit, though written from right to left, he assigns it to the Kabool valley and the Paropamisus,* which are known to have been peopled from India before the expedition of Alexander. The coins, with Sanscrit characters of the age of Asoka, he assigns to the country immediately bordering on the Indus, and to a period earlier than that of the adoption of the Arian language. A peculiar value

* The Paropamisus being peopled from India, may have received its alphabet from Assyria, which would account for the language being of Sanscrit, and the alphabet of semitic origin. In the tombs of Tuscan kings Greek has been found written in the same manner.

will attach to the bilingual Arian coins, if, through them, we succeed in completely discovering the language, of which they are the key, and so obtain, from inscriptions on rocks and relics, substantial evidence of dates and circumstances connected with the dynasties which used it. The late Mr. James Prinsep, whose perspicacity and laborious study had previously restored the language of the Indian kings we read of as corresponding and making treaties with Seleucus and Antiochus, has the principal merit of using the names found upon these coins, as a key for the discovery of the Arian alphabet, and of carrying it further into the titles, by which the kings who adopted the bilingual form of coinage chose to distinguish themselves; but in these researches he had several competitors, and in the assignment of values to letters, as well as in the ascertainment of the proper reading of the epithets and titles, he was sometimes, as we have before stated, rivalled, if not anticipated, by the learned of Europe. Much as has been done, however, in this particular line, we shall not think that discovery has reached its limit, until the inscriptions found in Arian characters upon rocks, and on the relics of topes and tumuli, are also decyphered; for it is through them only that we can hope to obtain a trustworthy historical record, to confute, or confirm, the conjectures which, at present, are our only guide in the dark obscurity produced by the indifference and neglect of western writers. The literature of ancient India has been searched in vain for facts and circumstances to illustrate this period. Sanscrit books are yet more destitute of historical notices, than those of classic Europe. A ray of doubtful light is, however, cast on the period by Chinese historians, and Professor Lassen has made good use of these authorities in the illustration of his theory of Scythian ascendancy: but it is only a lightening glimmer that we derive from that source, and it may prove deceitful in the deductions and inferences to which he has applied it.

Having noticed that the arrangement of the new kings, and the assignment of dates and territories to them, are built mainly on the varieties of the coins above briefly stated, we shall now follow Professors Lassen and Wilson through their chronological classification, and apply it to the known history of this part of Asia.

B.C. 256. The first THEODOTUS, or Diodotus, on whose coins we find the simple inscription, ΔΙΟΔΟΤΟΥ ΒΑΣΙΛΕΩΣ, is declared by Greek and Latin historians to have asserted his independence at the same time that, or a little before, Arsaces revolted in Parthia. If Strabo is to be believed, who says that Arsaces fled from Bulkh to Parthia, because the rival faction of Theodotus prevailed there, the revolt of Bactria may have been some years antecedent. The reign of Theodotus continued until after Arsaces had conquered Hyrcania, for the latter then feared a confederacy of the Bactrian with the Syrian king; he was, however, relieved from this fear by the death of Theodotus, and thereupon entered into strict alliance with his son and successor of the same name; from this circumstance we are led to a conclusion as to the date of his decease.

B. C. 240. THEODOTUS II. We have no certain knowledge of the character, actions, or fate of this king, nor do the few coins yet found afford any means of distinguishing between the father and son. The extent of their dominion is also uncertain. It is said, indeed, that the other Greek colonies of the further Asia, followed the example set by Bactria and Parthia: but whether Aria, Arachotia, and the Paropamisus, including Kophen, or the Kabool valley, ranged themselves under Theodotus, or chose their separate kings, is nowhere stated. We conclude that Theodotus held dominion over all the countries east of Parthia, because the name of no other revolting sovereign is anywhere mentioned, and we know that Arsaces I. had only Parthia and Hyrcania.

B. C. 220. EUTHYDEMUS. The coins have ΒΑΣΙΛΕΩΣ ΕΥΘΥΔΗΜΟΥ* on the reverse only, with a Hercules standing, or sitting. The only other reverse type is the wild horse of Bactria, with the same inscription. This king we find established at the time of the expedition of Antiochus the Great, which was

* See plate, No. 1.

undertaken in B.C. 212. He does not appear to have assisted in that king's war with Arsaces, but after the peace between them, he met in battle the united Syrian and Parthian forces, and was defeated. The battle must have been fought near Merv, where the ancient Antiochia is supposed to have stood. Enthydemus fled after it to Ariaspe. The situation of Hazarasp, across the desert, is precisely that to which, after such a defeat, the Bactrian king might be expected to retire.* Euthydemus had there the desert between him and the conquerors, with Soghdiana and the Scythians for a resource in his rear. His appeal from that place is said to have had great weight with Antiochus. He represented, that it was not he that had revolted from Syria; but, on the contrary, he had overpowered and displaced the family that was guilty of that act. That he personally, therefore, was entitled to favour rather than enmity. On the other hand, that it was for the interest of Antiochus as a Greek to strengthen and support, instead of weakening him, for that it was as much as the Greeks could do, to maintain themselves against the Scythians who had been called in by Arsaces. That by receiving him into alliance, Antiochus

* Strabo says that Arsaces fled in the same direction when hard pressed by Seleucus Callinicus, and was received and assisted by the Chorasmeni or tribes of Kharizm.

might restore the Greek dominion over the whole country held by the first Seleucus, that is to the Indus, which, if he wasted his resources in a Bactrian war, he would lose the opportunity of doing. These arguments, urged appropriately by the son of Euthydemus, Demetrius, a handsome youth, who found immediate favour, prevailed with Antiochus: and Euthydemus, obtaining favourable terms, led the Syrian army through Bactria, that is, by the route north of the mountains to the Kabool valley, and across the Indus, in B. C. 206. There Antiochus made the peace with Sophagasenus (Asoka), which we find referred to in the edicts of that sovereign, gazetted by inscription on rocks and pillars in various parts of India, in characters exactly resembling those on the coins of Agathocles.* In B. C. 205, Antiochus returned by Arachotia and Karmania, that is, by the route followed by Craterus when Alexander returned. We do not find that he met any where with difficulty or resistance: on the contrary, it is evident that the Greek colonists of this region regarded with satisfaction the advent of an army and king of their own race, and derived strength and increased authority from their passage

* See the translation of these edicts in the journals of the Asiatic Society, for March, 1838, by James Prinsep. That on the Girnâr rock specifically names Antiochus (*Antiochia yôna Raja*), as engaged to use his influence to prevent the slaughter of animals.

through the country. Professor Lassen supposes, on no ground, however, but that of probability, that Euthydemus, being left by Antiochus in possession of Bactria, may then, or subsequently, have added Kâbool to his dominions, with Herât, or Aria; and that Demetrius, to whom Antiochus gave his own daughter in marriage, was made governor of Arachotia, and Seestan, or Drangiana. Afterwards, when Antiochus fell into trouble, in consequence of his Roman war, the Professor supposes Demetrius to have assumed the regal title in his father's life-time, and to have extended his territory by the conquest of Sindh, Kutch, and Goozrat: for history mentions Demetrius as an Indian conqueror, and we have good reason to believe that Baroach and Surat fell at this period under Greek dominion.

B.C. 190. DEMETRIUS,* whose coins have ΔΗΜΗΤΡΙΟΥ ΒΑΣΙΛΕΩΣ, with more variety than those of Euthydemus on both obverse and reverse. Thus the head is sometimes filletted, and sometimes has a strange elephant head-cap, and on one coin the elephant's head stands on the obverse, in place of that of the king. On the reverse we find Hercules, Apollo, and Minerva all standing, and on one coin the caduceus of Mercury. The date of the decease of Euthydemus is not known. Professor Wilson places it in 190

* See Plates I. and V.

B.C. his date for the accession of Demetrius. We learn from Justin and other western historians, that Demetrius, after his father's death, contended with Eucratides for the dominion of Bactria, and the latter, being besieged with a few hundred followers, retrieved his affairs by his valour and conduct, and finally overthrew Demetrius, and recovered his dominions, including India. The passage contains almost all we know of this king, and of Eucratides, and shows the latter to have been cotemporary, in the time of his accession to power, with Mithridates the first, of Parthia, the date of the commencement of whose reign, we have assigned above, in the summary of Arsacidan kings, to the year 177 B. C. Much argument, however, is raised upon Justin's words, which are as follow:—

"Eodem fere tempore, sicuti in Parthis Mithridates, ita in Bactris Eucratides, magni uterque viri, regna ineunt. Sed Parthorum fortuna felicior ad summum hoc duce fastigium eos perduxit: Bactriani autem, per varia bella jactati, non regnum tantum, verum etiam libertatem amiserunt. Siquidem Sogdianorum, et Arachotorum, et Drangianorum, Indorumque bellis fatigati, ad postremum ab *invalidioribus* Parthis, velut exsangues, oppressi sunt. *Multa* tamen Eucratides bella magnâ virtute gessit, quibus attritus, quum obsidionem Demetrii *regis Indorum* pateretur, cum trecentis militibus sexaginta millia hostium assiduis eruptionibus vicit. Quintâ itaque mense liberatus, Indiam in potestate redegit. Unde quum se reciperet, a filio, quem socium regni fecerat, in itinere interficitur; qui, non dissimulato parricidio, veluti hostem non patrem interfecisset, et per sanguinem ejus currum egit, et corpus abjici insepultum jussit."

B.C. 178. EUKRATIDES. Notwithstanding the above direct evidence to the cotemporary accession of Eucratides and Mithridates, there is much diversity of opinion as to the precise date of both events. Bayer gives 181 B. C. and he is followed by Professor Wilson, Visconti 165 B. C., and Professor Lassen takes the mean of these two, 175 B.C. which brings the date close to that we have assigned to the Parthian king, whom, however, there is no ground whatever for considering to be the elder of the two. Professor Lassen allows ten years for the wars with Demetrius, which wore out Eucratides, and supposes him to have finally triumphed about the year 165 B. C. then to have made a separate expedition into India, upon return from which he was murdered by his son. The words of Justin, and his designation of king of the Indians, applied to Demetrius, lead to the inference, that this siege was endured during operations in that direction. But the country of the Indians included Kabool and the Paropamisus, and much territory also to the west of the Indus river, towards Arachotia; the expression, therefore, leads to nothing conclusive. Strabo adds to these particulars obtained from Justin, the cession of some provinces of western Bactria to Mithridates by Eucratides during his difficulties, and confirms the reported manner of his death upon return from India, and this is all we find in history about this great king.

The coins* of Eucratides discovered in Bactria and Afghanistan are very numerous, and the types and devices are various, betokening a long and eventful reign. We have some exactly like the coins of Demetrius and Euthydemus, with a filletted head only on one side, and the Greek inscription on the reverse, with an Apollo. In these Eucratides is simply styled king, ΒΑΣΙΛΕΩΣ ΕΥΚΡΑΤΙΔΟΥ. Others have a helmeted head on the obverse, without any inscription, and the Dioscuri mounted on the reverse, with the inscription in Greek, ΒΑΣΙΛΕΩΣ ΜΕΓΑΛΟΥ ΕΥΚΡΑΤΙΔΟΥ. This device of the Dioscuri, on their caps, is by far the most common of those found upon the coins of Eucratides, and is nearly universal when the head is helmeted.† Again, we have the same helmeted head with the Greek in-

* See Plate I.

† Not quite universal. See two coins in the supplemental plate of Wilson's Ariana Antiqua.

scription round it, and with an Arian inscription round the Dioscuri on the obverse, and this commonly on square coins, the words in Arian being *Maharajasa Mahatasa Eukratidasa.* There is, however, one very peculiar coin,* a tetradrachme, with the head of Eucratides on the obverse, and the words ΕΥΚΡΑΤΙΔΗΣ ΒΑΣΙΛΕΥΣ ΜΕΓΑΣ in the nominative case, while on the reverse there are two heads, male and female, with the words ΗΛΙΟΚΛΕΟΥΣ ΚΑΙ ΛΑΟΔΙΚΗΣ. Professor Wilson considers this to be a coin of Heliocles, because of this genitive case; but much the more natural construction seems to be, that ΥΙΟΣ is to be understood, and that the reverse gives the names of the king's father and mother, neither of whose heads, be it observed, is filletted, to denote royalty, and to neither name is there any title or epithet.

We deduce the following circumstances from these coins. First. That Eucratides ruled originally in Bactria, succeeding Euthydemus there, as supposed by Professor Lassen; for we have only pure Greek coins without the title of great king, whereas the Arian inscription is never found without this more ambitious title. Secondly. That this title of great king can only have been assumed after, and, perhaps consequently upon, conquests in, and south

* See Journal of Asiatic Society for July, 1838, page 638; also the additional plate in Professor Wilson's Ariana Antiqua.

of the Paropamisus, or in Kabool, and that Eucratides, then first of all the Greeks, coined with the bilingual Arian inscription. Professor Lassen, indeed, supposes Agathocles to have been his cotemporary, and to have risen with him on the death of Euthydemus, establishing himself in Kabool, and in the hills to the Indus, with possessions across the Hindoo Koosh, as far as the Oxus, and holding them until overpowered and driven out by Eucratides. In this case, the priority of bilingual coinage in this region must be assigned to Agathocles. But the second language of Agathocles was Sanscrit, of the character used by Asoka, not Arian, as on the coins of Eucratides; on which account, it seems not improbable, that Agathocles may have been left by Antiochus, as governor in Kabool, consequently upon the cession of some part of that territory by Asoka, the dominion of Euthydemus, being confined to the country north of the Hindoo Koosh. This, however, is only conjectural.

The passage cited from Justin, which speaks of many wars waged successfully by Eucratides, bears out the inference that he overpowered Agathocles. On the other hand, the profusion in which bilingual coins of Eucratides have been discovered in various localities, joined to the comparative rarity of Greek coins, with the simple title of king, seems to justify the further inference, that Eucratides obtained

Kabool and the Paropamisus at an early period; and further, that he must have driven Demetrius into India, and ruled Ariana, or Afghanistan, as well as Bactria and Kabool, some time before the war in which he endured the siege of five months, described by Justin, and ultimately overpowered and destroyed his rival. Then, at last, he conquered or recovered India, re-annexing it to his Bactrian and Arianian dominions, and so became sole king over the entire territory from Parthia to the Indus, including the Punjâb and Sindh, but was not so for any long period; for all authorities concur in declaring Eucratides to have met his death from the hand of his son, when on his march in return from this Indian expedition. No author, however, mentions either the son's name, or any circumstances that can be used to assist in determining the date of this occurrence. Justin declares the son to have been associated with his father on the throne, but we have yet lighted on no coins to support, or give evidence of such an association; for the double-headed coin, which might seem to imply this, has no fillet or royal insignia, nor title of king, even, for the head on the reverse.

B.C. 155. HELIOCLES.—ΗΛΙΟΚΛΕΟΥΣ ΒΑΣΙΛΕΩΣ ΔΙΚΑΙΟΥ. The parricide successor of Eucratides is by some supposed to have borne his father's name, Eucratides, but Professor Lassen, following Mionnet, thinks Heliocles the most probable of the kings yet discovered to have been this son, and Professor Wilson adopts the same conclusion, giving 147 B.C. for the date of his violent accession. The assumption of the title ΔΙΚΑΙΟΥ by Heliocles, is no obstacle, and if our interpretation of the double-headed coin be correct, there is the Grecian, as well as the Asiatic custom, of naming after the grandfather, in favor of this supposition. The coins* of Heliocles are found both pure Greek, and bilingual, which is against the supposition of their being coins of the father of Eucratides; but not so of the son, whose government, though short, will have extended, like that of his father, both over Bactria and the Paropamisus, where the Arian language was vernacular.

B. C. 150. ANTIMACHUS. ΑΝΤΙΜΑΧΟΥ ΒΑΣΙΛΕΩΣ, also ΑΝΤΙΜΑΧΟΥ ΒΑΣΙΛΕΩΣ ΘΕΟΥ, and ΒΑΣΙΛΕΩΣ ΝΙΚΗΦΟΡΟΥ. The figure on the reverse of the plain Greek coins is supposed to be a Neptune, but this seems very doubtful. Assuming Eucratides to have reigned 25 years, from 175 B. C. (Professor Lassen's date for his accession), his death will have occurred in 150 B.C. The Professor, however, gives him a reign of 15 years only, ending in 160 B.C. Dr.

* Plate, No. II.

Wilson, following Bayer, makes his reign extend from 181 to 147 B.C. P. Rochette makes this reign end in 155 B.C., and we incline to prefer this date, which is a mean of all these opinions. We know that Demetrius Nicator of Syria made his expedition against Parthia in 140 B. C., and was assisted in it by the Greek colonists of Bactria, then recently brought under the yoke of Parthia, which was disliked by them. Professor Lassen's supposition in respect to the date of the death of Eucratides—viz. 160 B. C., gives twenty years, while Bayer and Professor Wilson allow barely seven years for the rule of such other kings, as may have reigned in Bactria after Eucratides, before the period of its subjugation by Mithridates of Parthia; our date, 155 B. C., leaves fifteen years. Assuming, therefore, the coins of purely Greek device, with pure Greek names and titles, to be of Bactrian successors of Eucratides, there are only Heliocles, Antimachus, and Agathocles, who fulfil this condition, and the two former coined with bilingual inscriptions,* that is, Greek and Arian, as well as in Greek only, while the latter coined also with Greek and ancient Sanscrit legends. As he is supposed the earliest, and his case is peculiar, we must here introduce him.

* Plate, No. II.

B. C. 190. AGATHOCLES,* ΒΑΣΙΛΕΩΣ ΑΓΑΘΟΚΛΕΟΥΣ. *Agathoklayaja, Sans.* Professor Lassen considers this king, as we have before stated, to be the ruler of Kaboolistan to the Indus, with possessions across the Hindoo Koosh to the Oxus, and he supposes him to have been opposed to Eucratides, and conquered by him. PANTALEON, who also coined with Greek and Sanscrit legends, and of whom no coins of pure Greek device and inscription, or with Arian characters, have yet been found, he supposes to have succeeded Agathocles in the country near the Indus, not including Kâbool or Bulkh, which, from Agathocles had, he concludes, passed to Eucratides, and his successors. If this supposition be admitted, we have only Heliocles and Antimachus† for the period from the death of Eucratides to the conquest of Bactria by Mithridates, and both may well have reigned in that country and the Paro-

* Agathocles 190 to 165 B.C., Lassen. Professor Wilson places Agathocles in 135 B.C., but this seems to us to be inconsistent with the character of the pure Greek coins of this king, and with the simplicity of their style and title. Like Euthydemus and Demetrius, he has no epithet; neither has his supposed successor, Pantaleon, any title or epithet, but ΒΑΣΙΛΕΥΣ. This circumstance seems strongly in favor of Professor Lassen's conjecture, for the successors of Eucratides appear all to have coined with epithets, but none of his predecessors, nor himself.

† Professor Wilson gives 140 B.C. for the date of Antimachus, making him the successor of Heliocles; but this would be opposed to the fact of Mithridates' conquest of Bactria before that date.

pamisus in this interval, for we have no reason to suppose that either had long reigns. We see no occasion, therefore, to seek a separate kingdom for Antimachus in Drangiana, and the fact of his coins being found bilingual also, is against his being the immediate short-lived successor of Demetrius in that region, as supposed by Professor Lassen, for we have no bilingual coins of Demetrius. It would thus appear that the order of succession in such parts of Bactria as had not already been ceded to Mithridates of Parthia by Eucratides himself, was, first Heliocles, then Antimachus: The other Nikator and Nikephorus kings, may then have maintained a struggle with the Parthian king in Aria, and the Paropamisus, until 140 B.C. when all were subdued. Agathocles, however, was by half a century antecedent to these, and in a different region; viz., in Kabool. If our supposition be true, that he was the Governor left by Antiochus in Kabool after his treaty with Asoka, an earlier date by ten years, than that of Professor Lassen, might safely be assigned, for that of his asserting independence, and also for his making conquests over the Hindoo Koosh, if it be required to carry him there, in order to account for the Grecian purity of the silver coins of this king; but the early date alone will suffice for this, for the supposition makes him cotemporary with Demetrius.

B. C. 195. PANTALEON.* ΒΑΣΙΛΕΩΣ ΠΑΝΤΑΛΕΟΝΤΟΣ. *Pantalawanta*, Sans. Pantaleon, according to our hypothesis, might well be another Governor appointed by Antiochus to ceded territory, in which the official language of Asoka was in use. He may then have been overpowered by Agathocles, as probably as by Eucratides, being the cotemporary, not the successor of the former. Both these kings used the simple title of Basileus, without epithet or addition of any kind, which, with the perfect form of their Greek letters, is an evidence of antiquity. In their Sanscrit they gave the names only without any title.

Leaving, for the present, the kings of Bactria, Kabool, and Aria, whose coinage was Greek only, or Greek and Sanscrit, we must now bring on the stage the long list of Greek kings, whose coinage has been brought to light of pure Greek device, with an Arian inscription on the reverse, generally round some deity or object derived from the Grecian mythology. We have seen that Eucratides was the earliest of the kings who adopted this bilingual inscription, and we suppose him to have done so, consequently upon his conquest of the Paropamisus, we know it to have been after his assumption of the title of Great King. Upon the death of this king, his wide dominion is supposed to have been broken into several independent kingdoms, and the number of kings, great kings, and kings of kings,

* See Plate II., No. 4.

resuscitated by late discoveries, compared with the known date of Scythian conquest, would seem to require some such subdivision. Professor Lassen supposes three kingdoms, besides that of Bactria; one eastern under Menander and Apollodotus, comprehending the Punjâb and valley of the Indus with Kâbool, and Arachotia, or Kandahar, added in times of its prosperity. Another western, at Herât and in Seestân. A third central, of the Paropamisus, which latter region, however, we incline to give to Bactria, because of the bilingual as well as pure Greek coins of Heliocles and Antimachus kings of Bactria. Some such division of Afghânistan, as is here supposed, has commonly followed the break up of a dynasty of Afghân kings, and holds good at present in that country, consequently upon the dissolution of the monarchy of Ahmed Shah. The supposition, therefore, is not unreasonable, though without positive foundation in history.

For the classification, and assignment to these regions, of the kings resuscitated, we have very vague materials, or grounds for conjecture. Of these, the first is the continuance of the same or similar titles. We have, for instance, a long list of kings, all assuming the epithet ΣΩΤΗΡ or saviour, with the simple title of king (ΒΑΣΙΛΕΥΣ), and all using the Arian as well as Greek character and language, and not dissimilar devices and emblems on their coins. It is, hence, fair to presume that these were all of the same dynasty, though, of course, the inference is not conclusive, nor indeed generally admitted. The title ΣΩTHP is uniformly rendered into Arian by the same word, but it is one of the few that have not been satisfactorily read. The word for king is always Maharâjasa 𐨯𐨗𐨪𐨱𐨨, on this all are agreed, but for ΣΩTHP we have 𐨯𐨪𐨡𐨟, or 𐨯𐨪𐨟𐨟. Mr. James Prinsep read this *Nandatasa.* Professor Wilson reads it but doubtingly *Tadarasa.* Professor Lassen *Tâdâro* or *Tâdârasa,* for he altered his reading of the ô on learning that Mr. James Prinsep had found the last letter 𐨯 used for s. We incline to a later reading by Lieutenant Cunningham, of the Bengal Engineers, who finding the backward stroke of the first letter to be identical with that used with the k in Eucratides, reads the word *Tradâtasa,* thus identifying it more directly with the Sanscrit word Trân, protection. We have the nine following saviour kings:—

B. C. 155. 1. MENANDER.* ΜΕΝΑΝΔΡΟΥ ΒΑΣΙΛΕΩΣ ΣΩΤΗΡΟΣ.
B. C. 135. 2. APOLLODOTUS. ΑΠΟΛΛΟΔΟΤΟΥ ΒΑΣΙΛΕΩΣ ΣΩΤΗΡΟΣ, sometimes also, ΚΑΙ ΦΙΛΟΠΑΤΟΡΟΣ.
3. DIOMEDES. ΔΙΟΜΗΔΟΥ ΒΑΣΙΛΕΩΣ ΣΩΤΗΡΟΣ.

Cunningham. {
4. ZOILUS. ΖΩΙΛΟΥ ΒΑΣΙΛΕΩΣ ΣΩΤΗΡΟΣ.
5. HIPPOSTRATUS. ΙΠΠΟΣΤΡΑΤΟΥ ΒΑΣΙΛΕΩΣ ΣΩΤΗΡΟΣ.
6. STRATON. ΣΤΡΑΤΩΝΟΣ ΒΑΣΙΛΕΩΣ ΣΩΤΗΡΟΣ also ΚΑΙ ΕΠΙΦΑΝΟΥΣ.
7. DIONYSIUS. ΔΙΟΝΥΣΙΟΥ ΒΑΣΙΛΕΩΣ ΣΩΤΗΡΟΣ.
8. NICIAS. ΝΙΚΙΟΥ ΒΑΣΙΛΕΩΣ ΣΩΤΗΡΟΣ.
B. C. 120. 9. HERMÆUS. ΕΡΜΑΙΟΥ ΒΑΣΙΛΕΩΣ ΣΩΤΗΡΟΣ, (also ΕΡΜΑΙΟΥ ΚΑΙ ΚΑΛΛΙΟΠΗΣ)
}

We do not vouch for the order in which these

* See Plates III. and IV. for the coins of these Soter kings, those of Nicias and Dionysius only are wanting, having never yet been published.

kings are ranged, but all have similar titles, and as we have observed, not dissimilar devices on their coins; those of Hermæus, however, are much less perfect than the others, and on some of his coins the Greek letters are corrupted. As he is the last, the coinage of his name may, probably, have been continued by his barbarous conquerors, until Azes took the Indian title of king of kings, and issued money in his own name: of this more hereafter.

Professor Lassen supposes that these Saviour Kings were all successors of Menander, in the Punjâb, Kâbool, and down the Indus. We have added five new names to the list of kings of this class, known to Professors Lassen and Wilson, all which have been subsequently discovered, and published through the Journal of the Asiatic Society at Calcutta,* by Lieutenant Cunningham of the Bengal Engineers.

Hermæus, the last king of the series, is supposed by Professor Lassen to have been overpowered by Azes, about the year 120 B. C., which, assuming Menander to have succeeded Eucratides in 155 B. C.,† would give only thirty-five years for the

* Journal, 1842, page 130 to 137, vol. xi.

† Professor Wilson gives 126 B. C. for the date of Menander's accession, judging partly from the character of his coins, and partly in order to keep his conquests in India clear of those of Mithridates. This, however, is opposed to the Soter classification, which assumes Menander to have been the founder of a dynasty using that title; and we see no reason for placing so wide an interval between him and Eucratides, whose immediate successor he has heretofore been considered by many critics.

entire series. The coins of all, except of the two first and of Hermæus, are very rare; there is no reason, therefore, to infer that they had long reigns; and, if it were necessary to suppose a division of territory, in order to provide kingdoms for so many, the tract of country assigned to Menander and Apollodotus is wide enough to hold several petty sovereigns during a period of convulsion.

The augmentation of the number of Soter, or Saviour, kings affords, therefore, no argument against Professor Lassen's hypothesis in respect to their connection with the same regions, and the fact of Mithridates II. having penetrated as far as the Indus, is not opposed to the notion, that a Soter Greek sovereign may have held the territory beyond, and there preserved his independence.

Let us now take another series of Greek sovereigns with titles and epithets of a different character. We find three kings with the epithet ΝΙΚΗΦΟΡΟΥ, two with ΑΝΙΚΗΤΟΥ, and one ΝΙΚΑΤΟΡΟΣ, viz.*

I. ANTIMACHUS. ΑΝΤΙΜΑΧΟΥ ΒΑΣΙΛΕΩΣ ΝΙΚΗΦΟΡΟΥ (Arian) *Antimakhasa Maharajasa Jyadharasa.*

II. ARCHELIUS. ΑΡΧΕΛΙΟΥ ΒΑΣΙΛΕΩΣ ΔΙΚΑΙΟΥ ΝΙΚΗΦΟΡΟΥ. (Professor Wilson reads ΑΡΧΕΒΙΟΥ also). (Arian) *Archeliasa Maharajasa Dhamikasa Jyadharasa.*

III. ANTIALCIDES. ΑΝΤΙΑΛΚΙΔΟΥ ΒΑΣΙΛΕΩΣ ΝΙΚΗΦΟΡΟΥ *Antialikidasa Maharajasa Jyadharasa.*

1. LYCIAS. ΛΥΣΙΟΥ ΒΑΣΙΛΕΩΣ ΑΝΙΚΗΤΟΥ *Lisikasa Maharajasa Apatihatasa.*

II. PHILOXENUS. ΦΙΛΟΞΕΝΟΥ ΒΑΣΙΛΕΩΣ ΑΝΙΚΗΤΟΥ *Pilishinasa Maharajasa Apatihatasa.*

I. AMYNTAS. ΑΜΥΝΤΟΥ ΒΑΣΙΛΕΩΣ ΝΙΚΑΤΟΡΟΣ (Arian) *Amitasa Maharajasa Jyadharasa.*

---

* See Plate II. for the coins of all these.

We have for these Aria-proper, that is Herât and Southern Bactria, which we know were conquered by Mithridates in about 145 B.C. and occasionally over-run by the Scythians, also Seestân or Drangiana. Antialcides is placed by Professor Lassen in the Paropamisus and Arachotia, in about 160 B. C. which is his date for the death of Eucratides, and is supposed to have been followed there by Lysias,* while Antimachus, Philoxenus, Archelius, or Archebius, and Amyntas, are by the same Professor assigned to Herât and Drangiana, in the period from 165 to 145 B.C., that is, from the death of Demetrius, till the conquest of that country by Mithridates. All this arrangement is arbitrary: we would only observe, that the tract of country assigned to these kings being in perpetual war with Scythians, or with the Parthian king, the Greek colonists, who maintained the struggle with the invaders, may well be supposed, upon the occasion of some temporary success, to have taken titles and epithets boastful of the victory. These kings are all simply styled ΒΑΣΙΛΕΩΣ, with their distinctive epithets, we have amongst them no ΜΕΓΑΣ ΒΑΣΙΛΕΥΣ, nor ΒΑΣΙΛΕΥΣ ΒΑΣΙΛΕΩΝ, king of kings, their territory could, therefore, not have been extensive.

There is again another class of Greek sovereigns,

* Professor Wilson gives 174 B. C. for the date of Lysias' accession; 135 B.C. for those of Amyntas and Antialcides, and 130 B. C. for that of Philoxenus; Archebius he brings down to 125-120, B.C. but all these dates rest, like Professor Lassen's, on conjecture only.

who took peaceful titles, implying the possession of some popular virtue, without claim to the reputation of success in war. They are few in number, and one of them is a queen, viz.—

155 B. C. HELIOCLES. ΗΛΙΟΚΛΕΟΥΣ ΒΑΣΙΛΕΩΣ ΔΙΚΑΙΟΥ, sometimes Greek only, and sometimes with Arian, *Maharajasa Dhamikasa Heliaklyasa.* Plate II. figs. 3 and 5.

TELEPHUS. ΤΗΛΕΦΟΥ ΒΑΣΙΛΕΩΣ ΕΥΕΡΓΕΤΟΥ. (Cunningham.) Arian, *Telephasa, Maharajasa, Sukarmasa.* Plate III. fig. 2.

140 B. C. AGATHOCLEIA. ΑΓΑΘΟΚΛΕΙΑΣ ΒΑΣΙΛΙΣΣΑΣ ΘΕΟΤΡΟΠΟΥ. Arian. *Maharajasa, Midratasa, Mikasaklayasa.* Pl. III. fig. 1.

Heliocles, the supposed parricide successor of Eucratides, has before been adverted to. We have no facts or circumstances of any kind to guide conjecture as to the date or locality of the reigns of the other two. The queen is placed, by Professor Lassen, after Apollodotus and Diomedes, amongst the Indian Soter kings, but merely on conjecture. We would observe, that the Arian inscription marks all these as reigning south of the Paropamisus, while the simple Greek coins of the first-named indicate dominion also in Bactria, and this is all we can venture to infer respecting them.

The above recapitulation of names, disposes of all the mint-possessing kings of Greek name and origin, whose coins have yet come to light. We pretend not to arrange, nor to assign dates and kingdoms to them with any certainty, in the utter want of historical data, or materials of any kind. Of all the kings who followed Eucratides, Menander, and Apollodotus are the only two whose names are anywhere mentioned in classic authors, and they are so only incidentally, and not in a manner to show how they came to power, or where their capital was situated, or how long, over what regions, and when they reigned.

All we know for certain is, that all have reigned at some period of the second century before our era, in some part of Bactria, Ariana, or the Punjâb. For the style of coinage of each of these kings it is sufficient to refer to the annexed plates, in which coins of all will be found, except of Nicias and Dionysius, which, though reported, have not yet been published by Captain Cunningham. The style of execution, types, and emblems upon all are so entirely and exclusively Greek, that there is nothing in them to which to draw special attention, excepting the forms of letters in the names and titles of the Arian superscriptions. As has before been said, these, after for several years exercising the ingenuity of the learned of Europe and India, who were long doubtful whether to assign to them a Syrian, Zend, or Pahlavee origin, were at length determined to be Sanscrit; and the value of each letter has been now ascertained with a precision and certainty that leaves no doubt, so far as the interpretation of these particular legends goes. In the course of years, however, the Arian alphabet seems to have undergone a change, and the same forms are not to be recognised in later coins, nor the same epithets and titles; and the inscriptions discovered in topes are all in the less simple later character, to which we shall come presently. Before dismissing these coins, however, we must notice that numismatists extract some evidence as to the locality of mintage from the devices. Thus, the elephant and elephant's head on the coins of Demetrius, Menander, and Apollodotus, and also on those of Lycias and Heliocles, are considered as indicating dominion in India. So the humped bull of Philoxenus, Diomedes, and others; while the wild horse and double-humped camel are supposed to have exclusive reference to Bactria. Again, because the coinage of Bactria and Ariana is derived from that of the Syrian kings, who preceded Theodotus, an argument as to the date of reigns is sometimes deduced from a comparison of emblems and devices with those of the Seleucidan coins, as from the Jupiter in a chair of Hermæus, which first appeared in Syria on the coins of Alexander Zebina who died in 123 B.C., and so by a comparison of titles, as the Theus on the coins of Antimachus. We attach little value to such evidences, which, at best, are only collateral, and lead to nothing conclusive. Those, however, who take delight in them, and think that useful results can be obtained by such means, will find in the annexed plates which may be placed alongside of any of the works already published on Syrian coins, all the facilities they can desire for making the comparison. We have not, indeed, given every type of kings like Eucratides and Menander, whose coins are very various, and have been discovered in great numbers, but a sufficiency of each will be found in these plates to show the style and peculiarities of every one of the kings; and those who desire fuller evidence, must refer to Professor Wilson, or to the original pages of the Journal of the Asiatic Society of Calcutta. It would be vain, indeed, to endeavour to supersede the necessity for such reference in the case of those who desire thoroughly to investigate the subject.

Of the Greek kings above given, Hermæus is undoubtedly the latest. Of his coins it will be seen, that there are four distinct kinds: and the difference between them is so great, that some have supposed there to have been two, and even three kings of the name. There is first a coin of Hermæus with Kalliope his wife, having a double head on the obverse, and in execution and device in other respects corresponding with the coins of other kings of Greek race. Again similar coins have been found of Hermæus alone, both of silver and copper, with the inscriptions, both Greek and Arian, in characters evidently of the same age as those of other Soter kings. But by far the most frequent coins of Hermæus are of inferior execution, and of copper: and of these there are two classes, one with a sitting Jupiter on the reverse, and the other with a standing Hercules. Both have the king's filleted head on the obverse, with the inscription ΒΑΣΙΛΕΩΣ ΣΩΤΗΡΟΣ ΕΡΜΑΙΟΥ, the name being at the bottom. On the coins with the type of Hercules, however, there are frequently at the end of the word ΣΩΤΗΡΟΣ, or its corruption, ΣΤΗΡΟΣ, the two letters, ΣΥ, the meaning of which has puzzled every body. Though separated from the name, which, being at the bottom, commences from the left, these letters are by many supposed to be part of it, and Su-Hermæus is accordingly given as a different king. We prefer to interpret the ΣΥ as an abbreviation. But the most strange part of this Hercules coinage is, that the inscription in Arian on the reverse, round the figure of Hercules, no longer contains the name of Hermæus, nor the title Maharaja for king, nor the usual word for Soter, or saviour. The letters, indeed, are in the same simple form, with exception to a single, or doublecross, +, or ++, which, whether letter, or abbreviated monogram, or mere mark to shew where to commence and finish reading the superscription, is still undetermined. The other letters have all been read, but not with the same certainty as the simple titles of Hermæus's predecessors. They prove to be *Dhama*, ++, *rata*, *Kujulakasa Sabashakha*, *Kadaphasa*, and the self same inscription, verbatim, is found on coins with this Hercules device, having on the obverse a head like that of Hermæus, but with the name in Greek letters, ΧΟΡΣΟ ΚΟΖΟΥΛΟ ΚΑΔΦΙΖΟΥ, and also on coins with other strange names.

It would be premature to discuss here the relation of these barbarians with Hermæus, because we do not believe Kadphizes, or Kadphises, to have been his immediate successor. All that we deduce at present is, that the coinage of Hermæus was carried on long after his reign had closed, and was taken up, or suffered, not only by this Kadphises, but by some Parthians, as by Undopherres, or Gondophares; for we find this king, also, coining with an Hermæus-like obverse, and with the corrupted title of ΣΤΗΡΟΣ, derived from the Hercules coins of Hermæus, before he took the more ambitious title of great king of kings. We know, indeed, that in ancient times mints were not exclusively royal; but the privilege of coining, and especially of coining copper, was exercised by every city, enjoying freedom or municipal privileges. It will be in some subordinate mint of this description, that the Hermæus coinage was carried down, until the desire to gratify a new conqueror, or direct subjection to his rule, led to the substitution of his name, first in the vernacular dialect of the reverse, and at last on both sides of the coin.

We come now to the Scythian kings, who, following the Greeks, adopted their forms of money, that is, coined similar pieces, with superscriptions similar, and in the same languages, but inscribed on them their own names and titles, and varied the emblems and devices.

B. C. 135. Maues. ΒΑΣΙΛΕΩΣ ΜΑΥΟΥ; also ΒΑΣΙΛΕΩΣ ΒΑΣΙΛΕΩΝ ΜΕΓΑΛΟΥ ΜΑΥΟΥ. *Rajati-rajasa Mahatasa Máasa.* Some of the coins of this king are of a different type altogether from those of the Greek successors of Eucratides; but we find him at first coining with a type and simple inscription exactly similar to that of Demetrius;* then we find him bilingual, with the type of Straton and Apollodotus; and at last he comes forth in the full blaze of barbaric pride, calling himself great king of kings, and issuing a coin exactly like that of Azes, the Scythian. From these circumstances we are compelled to assign to him a date anterior to that conqueror, but so little antecedent as to be his ally, perhaps to have called him in to share the spoils of Bactria, and, after enjoying a short-lived divided sovereignty with him, to have yielded to the greater authority, and power of his associate. Our reasons for hazarding this conjecture regarding Maues are the following :—First. The name is not Greek, neither is it Parthian, nor Indian; he was most probably, therefore, a Scythian, the head of one of the tribes that broke into Bactria between 150 and 140 B. C. Secondly. His coining in the Greek style shows, that he must have been established somewhere in the first instance by Greek appointment, or at least with Greek concurrence, and the style of his Greek, and the forms of the letters, indicate an early date for such establishment. He may, with his tribe, have sold his services to different Greek sovereigns, or free cities, and so at one time coined

* See Plate IV. figs. 12 and 15.

with only Greek, and at another with Greek and Arian, because occupying territory where one or other form of coinage prevailed. His subsequent association with Azes is proved by the correspondence of his later coins with those of that king; and, by the extraordinary fact, that a coin with the name of Maues is in the possession of Dr. Swiney, which exactly corresponds in type with that of king Azes, numbered 14 in Plate VII. annexed. Now this coin is very peculiar; it exhibits the king with a trident, a Tartar weapon of war, setting his foot on a prostrate enemy, on the obverse; and has a figure in the midst of fruit-bearing trees, or shrubs, indicating plenty, on the reverse. It must be evident, that if such a coin was struck and issued at the same time by two kings, each bearing the same titles, it must have been designed and struck to celebrate a joint victory; perhaps one of the victories in which kings Phrahates and Artabanes of Parthia lost respectively their lives. More of this, when we come to speak of king Azes. We have to remark, that coins of king Maues are rare. James Prinsep knew but of two certain varieties, and a third with a Bactrian wild horse, came to him too late to be drawn and engraved (No. 1, Plate V). Professor Wilson notices seven types of coins of this king, and another has since been discovered by Capt. Cunningham (No. 13, Pl. IV.) There are thus nine ascertained varieties of coins of Maues; but of Azes more than thirty have been found, and he has twenty-five varieties of monogram.

B. C. 130. AZES. The greatest of Scythians was evidently king Azes, whose coins we find generally with plain distinct Greek characters on one side, and with perfect legible Arian on the other. The titles of this king are uniformly the same. In Greek ΒΑΣΙΛΕΩΣ ΒΑΣΙΛΕΩΝ ΜΕΓΑΛΟΥ ΑΖΟΥ. In Arian, *Maharajasa Raja-Rajasa Mahatasa Ayasa.* The types of his coins are very various.* We lose altogether the well-executed Greek bust, or head, but have on one side a horseman, armed with a spear, or holding out his wrist, in a hawking attitude: on the other side, male or female figures of various kinds, not referable to Classic mythology; or we have animals on the reverse, such as the humped bull, the lion or panther, a horse or elephant, or a Bactrian camel, and sometimes we find animals on both sides. Professor Lassen looks upon these varieties as marking the different provinces subject to Azes, and both he and Professor Wilson recognise in some of the figures Greek and Hindoo divinities, but we cannot admit the likeness. On the coin, for instance, which is common to Azes and Maues, there is what to us appears to be the king with a trident, setting

* See Plates VI. and VII. engraved by James Prinsep, and already published in the Journal of the Asiatic Society, vol. IV.

his foot on the neck of a prostrate enemy, on the obverse, with the Greek inscription. This Professor Lassen considers to be a Neptune setting his foot on a swimmer, because of the trident in the hand of the standing figure; while Professor Wilson regards the tridented figure, as Siva, and in the plate of this coin he gives horns to the figure under foot, which we cannot discover on two varieties of the coin, and so constitutes him an Asoor, or devil subdued. The inference, however, that this coin was intended to typify a victory is too obvious not to have struck this Professor, and in that we are agreed. But whatever these figures and the animals on other coins, may be intended to represent, all agree that there is a marked difference between the types and devices of king Azes, and the pure mythological devices of the Greek coins of preceding kings, showing a new dynasty and new race, if not also, as we suppose, a new religion.

Who, then, is this great king of kings, Azes, whose coins are so numerous, and so various? where and when did he live and reign? Professor Wilson inclines to consider him an Indian Boodhist, with a name derived from Sanscrit, meaning "The Unconquered" (*Ajaya*), and assigns him a date only fifty years before our era, making him the successor of Azilises, whom he places ten years earlier. Professor Lassen looks upon Azes as a Sacian

Scythian, who conquered the Kâbool valley in the time of the second Mithridates, and finally destroyed the kingdom of Menander and Hermæus, in about 120 B.C. Azilizes, he considers to be the successor of Azes, and supposes him, with others of the same dynasty, to have ruled in that quarter, and in the Punjâb, until defeated by the great Indian king, Vikramaditya, who, from Oojein, is known to have extended his empire to Kâbool about 56 B.C. Professor Lassen supports this hypothesis by Chinese authority, for he finds it recorded in the histories of that nation, that the Szu Tartars, whom he identifies with the Sacæ, were expelled from the Ili valley by the Yuetchi, or White Huns, whom he supposes to be the Tochari,* about the year 150 B.C. After occupying Tahia, or Soghdiana, for a time, they are further stated by the Chinese, to have been driven thence also some years afterwards, and to have then established themselves in Kipen,† in which name he recognises the Kophen valley or Kâboolistan. This is a bold conjecture of Professor Lassen's, but we incline to think it a happy one, so far as concerns the date and manner of Scythian

* The name Tochari, or Thogari, is more like that of the Turks, or of the Yuegurs, who expelled the Yeutchi, and Professor Wilson recognises the Getæ in the name Yeutchi.

† Professor Wilson places Kipen in Soghdiana on the authority of the Chinese travellers, who, when entering India from Balti, state Kipen to be to the North. It does not, however, clearly appear from what point Kipen lay north, and we incline to take the similarity of name for a proof of identity.

dominion in Kâbool, and susceptible of support from classic, as well as from Tartar authority. The name Szu, with its varieties Se, Sai, and Anszu, may however, as it seems to us, be derived from Azes, or Azou, and be the same as the Asii and Asiani, rather than as the Sacæ of Strabo and Justin. Professor Lassen quotes from Strabo the following passage :—Μαλιστα δε γνωριμοι γεγονασι τῶν νομαδῶν, οι τους Ἑλληνας αφελομενοι την Βακτριανην, Ἀσιοι η* Ασιανοι, και Τοχαροι, και Σακαραυλοι, κτα. Now this passage, we think, may be construed thus: "The most famous and best known of the Nomades, were the Asii, or Asiani, who took Bactria from the Greeks, and the Tochari, and Sakarauli," &c., which Asii and Asiani, we conceive to mean the Scythians of king *Azes*. This construction seems to us much supported by the extract from the Prolegomena of Trogus Pompeius, also cited by the same Professor, "*Additæ res Scythicæ, reges Tocharorum Asiani*, &c., which we render; "to which are added the affairs of Scythia, and the kings of the Tochari, of the *Azes race and dynasty*." The Asii and Asiani are never mentioned by Herodotus, nor named in history as a tribe or nation, until we find them the destroyers of the Greek power in Bactria, and furnishing kings to the Tochari; nor are they traceable after this event as a nation. Not so the Sacæ, Getæ, and other tribes, the names of which are

* We have adopted here the amended reading of Vaillant, η Ασιανοι for Πασιανοι. The Pasians are never mentioned again, but the name Asiani is very generally used, as of the same tribe with the Asii, conquerors of the Greeks in Bactria.

found in various ancient authors of previous and subsequent ages. If, then, the Scythians under Azes are indicated as the Asiani, who overpowered the Grecian dynasties in Soghdiana and Northern Bactria between 140 and 130 B.C., or say about 135, B.C. we must allow for an interruption of these conquests by the Parthian kings, who held sway in Bactria as far as Bulkh, until the defeat and death of kings Phrahates and Artabanes in 130 B.C., after which Mithridates II. made some composition with the invaders; consequently the date assigned by Professor Lassen, viz., 126 B.C., will be nearly the time required for the final establishment of the Scythian dynasty by the conquest of Kâbool: and the series of victories that achieved such a conquest, would justify the great titles assumed by the king after its completion. We have no coins of Azes with less pretension than as "great king of kings," and none without the Arian superscription. This coinage, therefore, followed the expulsion of the Parthians, from Bactria, and the final overthrow of the Greek power in Afghanistan; but we do not draw from this fact an inference opposed to the supposition, that Azes may himself, in association with king Maues, have been the conqueror of Bactria also.

If, however, the Asii and Asiani are to be understood as meaning the Scythian, or Szu Nomades, who obeyed king Azes, it is clear that he united under him many tribes besides the Tochari and the Sacæ, in like manner as other Tartar conquerors of later day have done. The title "king of kings" is of itself evidence of this; the Sacians, therefore, can have had no exclusive property in such a sovereign, as supposed by Professor Lassen. Their settlement, first in the Kâbool valley, and afterwards, consequently upon fresh convulsions, in Seestan, or Sajistan, is an hypothesis that may or may not be true, quite independently of the general sovereignty of king Azes, and his conquest of Kâbool, or the Kophen valley, in 126 B.C., as stated by Chinese historians. Let us now see how the existence of such a sovereignty is supported by other Tartar authority, than that derived from Chinese history.

Abool Ghâzi Khan's genealogical History of the Tartars is the only work of the West, in which the traditions of these Nomade tribes have been collected. We there find, that a king named Oghus (*Ooghooz*) Khan, اوغوزخان warred successfully for a long time against other tribes, until he established amongst them, at last, sufficient authority to attack Itbarak Khan, of Kashghur, and Khotun. Being worsted at first, he renewed the war, and in the end conquering this king also, put him to death. "Then returning by the frontiers of India towards Talash, Saram, and Tashkund, he took these places, and sent his son to reduce Toorkestan and Andejan (on the Jaxartes), which he effected in six months. Then Oghus Khan advanced towards Samarkand, and conquered that place, and Bokhara. Next he took Bulkh, and in the middle of winter crossed the mountains to Chor, (Charikar ?) suffering much from snow and frost.

Here he wintered, and reviewed his army in the spring, and then marched against Kâbool, Ghuzni, and Kashmeer, where reigned a king named Jagma (Hermæus?), who maintained himself in mountain positions for a year, but was in the end defeated and slain. Oghus Khan then returned to Samarkand by Budukhshan, and sent an expedition westward against Khorasân, &c."

Now the line of this series of conquests corresponds exactly, with that required for the overthrow of the Greek power in Eastern Bactria and Kâbool, and is quite consistent with the retention by Mithridates II. of Western Bactria, that is Merv, Herât and Seestân, with which they would not interfere. The history proceeds, that advantages were gained over Parthia afterwards, because of the king's death, and the nonage of his successor, which also tallies with the accounts of the confusion in Parthia, and increase of Scythian audacity after the death of Mithridates II. The Tartar tradition, however, gives no help to chronology, for it assigns to Oghus Khan a reign of 116 years, and a date four thousand years before Chungeez Khan, whereas twelve hundred years is a sufficient period to have intervened between the two. In support of the hypothesis, that Oghus Khan may have been the great king of kings, Azes, we have, besides the similarity of name and of conquests, a curious coincidence; viz., that the Asii or Attasii, whom we suppose to be the Azes Nomades, are called also Augasii by Strabo, and Auzasii by

Ptolemy, who places them in the valley of Kashghur, precisely where Abdool Ghazi Khan says Oghus Khan defeated Itbarak before entering Bactria. In one of these appellatives, we have the name of Oghus transferred to the tribes he ruled, and in the other, that of the Azes of our coins clearly handed down for the same Nomade tribes. We think, consequently, this Tartar tradition, as given by Abdool Ghazi Khan, and confirmed by these names of tribes in Strabo and Ptolemy, affords as good a basis for a theory, in identification of the Azes of our coins, who supplanted the Greek sovereigns of Bactria and Kâbool, as the Chinese, not very distinct account, of the migration of the Szus and Youtchi. The Chinese account is, in fact, not at variance with, but rather supports our theory, especially if we are warranted in considering the name Szu, to be the Chinese corruption of the AZOΥ of our coins, with which it bears a remarkable similarity. Having thus found a place in history for king Azes, let us proceed with his successors.

B. C. 115. AZILISES.—ΒΑΣΙΛΕΩΣ ΒΑΣΙΛΕΩΝ ΜΕΓΑΛΟΥ ΑΖΙΛΙΣΟΥ. *Maharajasa Raja-Rajasa Mahatasa Ayalishisa.**

Azilises coined with the same titles as Azes, and with similar bilingual superscriptions, and devices, and these are continued down to some illegible names,† showing evidently a continuance of the dynasty in the country, where the Arian language was in use along with Greek.

* Plate VII., Nos. 27 and 28. † Plate V. fig. 2.

On one coin noticed by Professor Wilson, the name of Azes is on the Greek obverse, and Azilises on the Bactrian reverse, which we regard as evidence of a direct succession. Professor Lassen's hypothesis, that the dynasty of Azes ruled in the Punjâb, and Kâbool, until subverted by Indian conquest in the middle of the century before our era, seems rational: and that the successors of Azes had not the same extended sway, nor length of reign, with the founder of the dynasty, is evidenced by the smaller number, and greater uniformity of their coins.

In the summary we have given of the Arsacidan kings, it will be seen, that there was an interregnum of civil war and doubtful sovereignty, after the death of Mithridates II., that is in the early part of the century before our era. At this period we know the Scythians to have overrun Bactria, and there is, as we have shown, every reason to believe that they were established under Azes, and Azilises, in Kâbool and the Punjâb, and perhaps in Arachotia, and the Paropamisus also. We know, moreover, that the Parthian sovereignty was restored with Scythian aid, and had sufficient vitality, to subsist for two centuries and a half more in its western capital on the Tigris. It is, therefore, impossible to suppose that, during this interregnum of anarchy, Parthian satraps yielded every where their delegated power, and retired, without a struggle, to make way for Scythians. The more natural supposition is, that many asserted, and some maintained, their independence, in the territories over which they were placed with delegated sovereignty by Mithridates. To Azes, the great king of kings, many perhaps yielded a nominal, or real fealty; and Azilises also may have maintained himself as general sovereign; but after him, we find Parthians reappearing with a style of coinage, so nearly resembling that of Azes and Azilises, that we feel compelled to regard them as successors of these Scythian kings, and to fix the period from 90 to 60 B.C. for their reigns. Vonones, who, in his Arian legend, is called Balahara, seems to be the nearest successor to Azilises. Then we have Spalirisus, then Spalyrius, the brother of the king, and son of Balahara, according to the Arian legend. These three Parthians must have reigned in the Kâbool valley, and Punjâb, for there it is that their coins are found, and not rarely. We may suppose them to have made the conquest of Kâbool from Aria (Herât), or Arachotia, which were more properly Parthian satrapies; but the style of their coins forbids our assigning them a later date.

Professor Lassen considers it to be established, from the little we have of Indian history, that Vikramadiya, the fabulous hero of that country's romance, conquered Kâbool about the middle of the century before our era. We have the date of this king's reign, from the Sumbut era still current in India, which is 56 years earlier than our own. No coins have yet been discovered of Indian type and superscription, that could reasonably be assigned to a king of Oojein; but there is evidence of Indian interposition in the affairs of Kâbool, and the Punjâb. Professor Wilson, indeed, makes Azes Indian, as we have already noticed, and finding earrings, and Kshatrya caste-marks, on the head and bust of the obverse of the coins of the great Soter Megas, "king of kings," sets him down also as an Indian. Kadphises, too, coined with devices of Siva, and the bull, Nandi, in supercession of his original coinage with the name of Hermæus, and the Hercules type. This king the Professor also regards as Indian or Indo-Scythian. Jas. Prinsep, in one of his papers, threw out the idea that Gondophares might have some connexion with Gandharupa, the father of Vikramaditya, giving to the name a derivation from ΦΑΡΟΣ *pallium*, meaning the "wild-ass-skin-cloaked," to connect it with the fable of that conqueror's parentage. All these theories are ingenious, and some very plausible; still it is evident, that we have yet to trace, or verify, Vikramaditya. The fact of the Soter Megas having coined so largely with a Greek legend only, is conclusive against the notion of his being an Indian. Both Mr. James Prinsep, and Professor Lassen, indeed, considered it to be established, that this Soter Megas, king of kings, coined exclusively with a Greek legend on the reverse, and never with Arian. The coin, No. 23, plate VII., which has the peculiar monogram of Soter Megas, [monogram], they assign to Azes, whose name the former thought he discovered in the Arian legend. Of this coin there are three perfect specimens in the Masson collection at the India House, and they do not verify the reading of *Ayasa*, for the letters under the standing figure on the reverse. Professor Wilson, who gives two engravings of the same coin, assigns it on this account to Soter Megas, whose inscription, "great saviour king of kings," without any name, is clearly legible on the obverse. This discovery of a Soter Megas coin, so like in type to those of Azes, and with an Arian legend on the reverse, destroys much of the theory, which placed him in Soghdiana and Bactria, at the period when Azes ruled in Kâbool. His Greek is evidently of a later period than that of Azes, Azilises, Onones, Spalirisus, and Spalyrius; but it is purer than that of Undopherres, Abagasus, Abalgasius, and that set of Parthians. We are disposed, on this account, to assign him a date intermediate, that is, cotemporary with Vikramaditya, and anterior to Kadphises, and Kadphes Koranos, and the seat of his power will have been Bactria, Soghdiana, and the Paropamisus. This date for the Soter Megas, king of kings, differs from that assigned to him by Professor Wilson, in so far as it places him after, instead of before, Vonones. This Professor also has reversed the order we have given to Azes, Azilises, Spalyrius, and Spalirisus, besides excluding Vonones from the list. Our classification places them as follows.

B. C. 100. VONONES.* ΒΑΣΙΛΕΩΣ ΒΑΣΙΛΕΩΝ ΜΕ-

* See Plate VIII., figs. 1, 2, and 3.

ΓΑΛΟΥ ΟΝΩΝΟΥ. *Maharajasa Dhamikasa Balaharasa.* It seems to us quite impossible to ascribe this coinage to either of the kings of the name of Vonones, whose names are in the Arsacidan list. He will have been a satrap, therefore, who asserted independence, and created himself a kingdom out of the dominions of Azilises, whose style of coinage, it is evident, that he continued.

B.C. 85. Spalirisus.* ΒΑΣΙΛΕΩΣ ΒΑΣΙΛΕΩΝ, ΜΕΓΑΛΟΥ ΠΑΛΙΡΙΣΟΥ. *Maharajasa Mahatakasa Palirishasa.* There is no king on the Arsacidan list, whose name is at all like Spalirisus; there is, therefore, no difficulty in setting him down, as an independent sovereign of Parthian extraction. His name is sometimes read Ipalirisus.

B.C. 75. Spalypius. ΣΠΑΛΥΡΙΟΥ ΔΙΚΑΙΟΥ ΑΔΕΛΦΟΥ ΤΟΥ ΒΑΣΙΛΕΩΣ. *Balahara Putasa Dhamikasa Spalapharmasa.* There are many coins of this Parthian, but none in which he calls himself king. For a long time the legend was read, as of a king Adelphortes, but the Arian confirms the fact, that he was only a vice-regent, son of Vonones, and perhaps brother of Spalirisus.

B.C. 70. The nameless great Soter king,‡ on whose coins we find, in rather corrupt Greek, on the reverse always when there is a bust on the

* Plate VIII., fig. 4. † Plate VIII. fig. 5.

‡ Plate VII., figs. 23 and 26; Plate IX., figs. 1, 2, and 3.

obverse, ΣΩΤΗΡ ΜΕΓΑΣ ΒΑΣΙΛΕΥΣ ΒΑΣΙ-ΛΕΩΝ. Of this king, as before observed, there are coins with an Arian legend, which James Prinsep and Professor Lassen ascribed to Azes. On all we find a peculiar monogram, with three prongs, the purport of which has not been discovered. With the addition of a prong, the same monogram was continued in coins of Kadphises, and of the Kanerkis, but it is not found in those of the Hercules type, derived from Hermæus. We consider the Soter Megas to have been cotemporary, but not identified, with Vikramaditya, and, notwithstanding the ear-rings, we do not think he is established to have been Indian.

But we have another series of Scythian coins, with no Arian inscription, and differing in other respects from those of the Azes dynasty. These have the name of Kodes, Hyrkodes,* and several other names, not decypherable, and not of Greek origin, or extraction, though found written in Greek characters only, more or less corrupt. Professor Lassen, confining Azes as king of the Szu, or Sakas, to the Kâbool valley, and Punjâb, upon Chinese authority, supposes the Tochari tribe to be the Yeutchi, and places them with their *Asian* kings, in Upper Bactria and Soghdiana, towards the end of the second century before Christ, at which period he gives western Bactria to the second Mithridates.

* See Plate V.

These coins, and others similar, of which the names have not been made out, but on which there is no Arian inscription, he assigns to these Scythians at that period. Professor Wilson, on the other hand, places Kodes amongst the Indo-Parthians. We think that the exclusive use of Greek for the inscriptions, defective as they are, on these coins, fixes their locality in Bactria or Soghdiana, north of the Imaus, and Paropamisan range, and precludes the supposition that they were Indian. But there is nothing whatsoever to guide us, in the assignment of these coins to any particular race of Scythians, or to any period of time. The comparative corruption of the Greek letters leads to the inference, that these Greek Scythians followed Azes, instead of preceding him, and so, ruling the tribes of Bactria and Soghdiana, were cotemporary with his direct successors in Kâbool, and the Punjâb. There is, on the reverse of the great Saviour's coins, the same mounted cavalier in a hawking attitude, that we find on the coins of Azes; the naked or wild horse of Bactria, or a horse's head, is the common type of these unascertained Greco-Scythians, and is an older device. The title " king of kings" assumed by the ΣΩΤΗΡ ΜΕΓΑϹ, and also carried down by the Kadphises kings, is likewise of later date though indicating extended dominion: the nameless kings, with Kodes,therefore,although mere local chiefs,such as now rule at Khoolum, Koondooz, and Bulkh, will have preceded the conquest of the Punjâb, and Kâbool by Vikramaditya, whose era, 56 years before Christ, dates from a victory obtained over Scythians in the Punjâb. India affords nothing but fables of the exploits of this great king; but Professor Lassen has discovered, in a passage of the Periplus, a confirmation of the fact of his conquests, and general sovereignty; for, with reference to the city of Ozene, which can be no other than Oojein, it is stated, that the ancient royal residence was there. This, as the Professor pertinently remarks, can only refer to the reign of Vikramaditya, all other general sovereigns of India having had their capitals at Palibothra in Behar, or at Kanouj, and Hustanapoora, on the Ganges, and Jumna. The want of coins, or inscriptions, of this Indian king, is much to be deplored; the more so, as we have in the pillar and rock inscriptions of Asoka, his predecessor by a century and a half, such undeniable evidence in support of what we find recorded of that king in Boodhist chronicles. A similar much desiderated testimony of Vikramadity may eventually be discovered by the researches of future archæologists, and after witnessing what has been done in respect to the great Asoka, we should be wrong indeed to despair. At present, we can only notice the hiatus occasioned by this Indian conquest, in the series of our Arian and Kâboolian dynasties. The recent numismatic discoveries afford, however, evidence of this Indian conquest, in the fact, that, after this period, we find Hindoo deities substituted for those of Grecian mythology, and most so in the coins of those kings, who are supposed to have followed nearest to his reign. To these we will now proceed.

Vikramaditya's dominion in the Kâbool valley cannot have been lasting. His empire in India even fell to pieces after his decease, and nearly a century elapsed before Chandrasena restored the sovereignty of Hindoostan in its unity; his death, therefore, must have left his trans-Indus conquests at the mercy of Scythian and Parthian adventurers. Professor Lassen fixes the rise of Kadphises at this period; Professor Wilson places him half a century later. As we recognize at least three kings of the Kadaphes, or Kadphises dynasty, their rule in the Kâbool valley may cover both periods. The earliest Kadphises, or Kadphizes will, of course, be the king, whose name is found on the Arian reverse of the Hermæus coins of Hercules type, and again with the same reverse, and a head on the obverse, having the inscription in corrupt Greek, ΚΟΡΣΟΧΟ, ΚΟΖΟΥΛΟ, ΚΑΔΦΙΖΟΥ. At this time the chief had probably not assumed the regal title; for we find neither ΒΑΣΙΛΕΩΣ on the obverse, nor its corresponding, *Maharajasa*, in the Arian of the reverse. Further, we find nothing indicative of any settled religion; for the Hercules worship was readily borrowed by wild Scythians from the Greeks, as a mere reverence of physical strength. Tacitus notices that Gotarzes, of Parthia, took up that worship from the Scythians; it was, therefore, common amongst them. In the district of the first rise of Kadphises, which we suppose to be the Kohistan, while Kâbool and its valley were subject to Indian rule, the chief seems to have retained his Scythian title, and rude worship of Hercules. Afterwards, overpowering the Indian governors, who followed Vikramaditya in the Kâbool valley, and Punjâb, he, or his descendants, seem to have adopted the Hindoo religion. For when their power was fully established, we find the kings, dropping their Scythian style, and coining with the Greek titles of their predecessors, in their most arrogant form, viz., ΒΑΣΙΛΕΥΣ ΒΑΣΙΛΕΩΝ ΜΕΓΑS, and ΒΑΣΙΛΕΥΣ ΒΑΣΙΛΕΩΝ, ΣΩΤΗΡ ΜΕΓΑΣ, and after assuming this lofty title, we find a Kadphises king to be the first coiner of gold, in which coinage, as well as in the copper, and silver pieces of the same type, Siva in the mixed male and female character, and very generally accompanied by the Bull, Nandi, is uniformly substituted for the deities of the Grecian mythology. At this time, therefore, the Hindoo Brahminical religion had become the state religion of the countries subject to the great king of kings, Kadphises, consequently upon the complete establishment of his sovereignty, in the place of the Indian successors of Vikramaditya. In the time of Augustus Cæsar, a letter in Greek was received at Rome from a king Porus, on the Indus, praying for assistance, and good offices. This Indian king, we conceive, not improbably to be the Hindoo Raja, expelled by Kadphises, which would allow a period of half a century for the full growth of the power of this race of kings. The fast increasing corruption of the Greek letters on the Kadphises coins, is consistent with the notion of a gradual rise of power, extending over a period of this duration, and cotemporaneous with the reign of Augustus Cæsar; that is, ending with the commencement of our era.

Professor Lassen, seeking from Chinese history some means of illustrating the rise of this Kadphises dynasty, finds it stated that Khioutchi-ouhi, or Kiutsui-Kio, a Yuchi, or Yeutchi, White Hun (which race he considers to be the same as the Tochari, or Turks, but Professor Wilson considers to be the Getæ), conquered the Szus, or Azes Scythians, in about 40 B.C., and dying at the advanced age of 84 years, his son Yenkao-ching, prosecuted his career of victory, and reduced the Indus valley, and Punjâb to subjection, in about 20 B.C. The time and circumstances of these conquests correspond exactly with what we suppose to be the career of the Kadphises kings; but the names are sadly metamorphosed, and scarcely recognizable. It is time, however, to lay before the reader the numismatic testimony that we possess, and which, as before stated, we consider as establishing the existence of three kings of this race.

50 B.C. KORSOKO KOZOULO KADPHISES (Arian) *Dhama* ⟊ *rata Kujulakasa Sabashakha? Kadaphasa.* The inscriptions on these coins have been ascertained by the collation of many specimens: we have given two of the most per-

fect, in the annexed plates, No. 7, Plate IV.; and No. 9, Plate IX. The reading of the Arian inscription is not yet quite conclusive, nor have we any satisfactory explanation of it. The name, Kujula Kadphes, seems established, and it is worthy of remark, that on none of the coins of Hercules type, is there any monogram, or emblem, to connect the coinage with that of other known, or supposed, Scythians. With Hermæus alone is there the slighest link of connection, not so with other coins of this name and race, as will be presently seen.

20 B.C. Zathos Kadaphes Khoranos, ΖΑΘΟΥ, ΚΑΔΑΦΕΣ ΧΟΡΑΝΟΥ. The Arian legend is not yet settled, for though many specimens of this coinage have been discovered, all are defective at the same part. Like the first Kadphizes, or Kadphises, this king placed his head, or bust, on the obverse, with a Greek legend,* and the head is filletted, to denote royalty, though the title ΒΑΣΙΛΕΥΣ is wanting. On the reverse is a sitting figure, with the arm extended, and wearing a loose flowing Indian dress; but whether the figure is mythological, Hindoo, or Greek, is not apparent. Professor Lassen inclines to think ΖΑΘΟΣ, and ΧΟΡΑΝΟΣ, to be titles, but, whether titles, or names, they clearly distinguish this king from his predecessor, Korso Kojoules, of the Hermæus, and Hercules type, besides which,

* See Nos. 4 to 8, Plate IX.

the Zathos coins have on them monograms corresponding exactly with those on the Azes coins, No. 22, Plate VII.; and No. 8, Plate VIII., which would seem to indicate, that the Kadphises rule, under the Zathos sovereign, had been extended over some new district of the kingdom of Azes. It is clear, that the Siva worship had not been yet established as the state religion of this dynasty.

5 B.C. VOHEMO KADPHISES. ΒΑΣΙΛΕΥΣ ΒΑΣΙΛΕΩΝ ϹΩΤΗΡ ΜΕΓΑΣ ΟΟΗΜΟΚΑΔΦΙϹΗϹ, sometimes OONMO, and OOKMO, from corruption of the letters. The entire inscription is found on copper coins,* having on the obverse the king, standing, in a Tartar dress, with coat, boots, and cap, his right hand pointing downwards to an altar, or pile of loaves, and having a trident separate on one side, and a club on the other. The reverse has the Siva, and Nandi bull, not mistakeable. One silver coin only of Kadphises has yet been found, having the same inscription omitting the word Soter. The gold coins† of this king, with the same reverse, or with Siva alone, without Nandi, have the bust of the king, with the Tartar cap, or the king sitting on a throne of state, or the king in his chariot drawn by two horses and the Greek legend is simply ΒΑΣΙΛΕΥΣ ΟΟΗΜΟΚΑΔΦΙϹΗϹ.

On all the coins, whether of gold, silver, or

* See Plate IX. No. 10.

† See Plate IX. No. 11; and Plate X.

copper, which have the title ΒΑΣΙΛΕΥΣ, there is to be found the monogram, , which corresponds with the monogram on the coins of the nameless ΣΩΤΗΡ ΜΕΓΑΣ, except that it has four, instead of three prongs; and on most of them we find a further monogram, , borrowed from the undecyphered coin, given as No. 2, Plate V., which has on the obverse a mounted warrior, and on the reverse a Hercules, crowned by two figures, one a winged victory. The Arian legends, on the reverse of all the Kadphises coins of this class, have been carefully collated, and contain several new letters which are variously decyphered. Mr. James Prinsep read the entire inscription, thus—*Maharajasa Rajadhi Rajasa Sabatracha ihacha Mahiharasa dhi Makadphishasa Nandata.* On some coins, however, he found before the name, *Saballasa Saviratasa Mahichhitasa,* and on the gold coins, *Vavahima Kadphisasa,* corresponding with OOHMO, before the same name in Greek. The meaning of this legend, as first given, he rendered "Of the great sovereign, king of kings, everywhere seizing the earth, Dhima (or Vohima) Kadphises, the saviour." Professor Lassen adopts this reading, modified so as to make Vahima always correspond with the Greek OOHMO. Professor Wilson reads *Maharajasa Rajadhi Rajasa Sabatraphativahama ha varaha Kapsisasa dhanasa;* but he is not sure of this reading, and bases it on the unique silver coin of this king. He does not attempt the translation.

The only thing certain we gather from these

readings is, that wherever ΒΑΣΙΛΕΥΣ is on the Greek obverse, Maharaja is to be found in the Arian legend of the reverse, and not otherwise; which seems to prove, that the regal title was not assumed, until the issue of the gold coinage, with its corresponding silver, and copper pieces. Korso Kozoulo, Koranos, and Zathos, therefore, if titles, were something short of royalty. Assuming the gold coinage to have been issued about the period of our era, there are sufficient varieties forthcoming, to indicate, either one long reign, or a succession of princes, using similar titles and types, and extending for the period of half a century. Professors Lassen and Wilson carry the dynasty of Kadphises through the whole of the first century of our era, and then consider it to have been overpowered by a fresh swarm of Scythians, under the Kanerki kings. There is evidence, however, to a partial restoration of the Greco-Parthian sovereignty, which, though not very authentic, is not to be lightly set aside. Philostratus, in his account of Apollonius Tyaneus, describes this religious pretender, as leaving the court of the Parthian king, Bardanes, in order to travel to India by the northern route, through Bactria, said then to be the easier; and the journey is given with such particulars, as must have been the result of enquiry. Upon crossing the Indus to Taxila, Apollonius found a king established there, who conversed with him in Greek, and whose name was Phrahates. His territory, it is expressly stated, extended to the passes, from the valley of

Kâbool, into Bactria. Now, though this account of Apollonius was written in the time of Severus, a century after his death, and is a tissue of lies, put together to deceive the world, still, such a fact, as that a king Phrahates reigned in the Punjâb, and Kâbool valley, contemporaneously with Bardanes of Parthia, would not have been stated, if, at the time of writing the history, such had not been the received notion; and if, in the age of Severus, such a piece of information was generally received, and believed, we surely cannot, at this late period, reject it as unfounded. On the contrary, we have in the coins of Undopherres and Gondophares, who both called themselves Phrahata in their Arian legends, a confirmation of the fact that, Phrahates was not an imaginary king. The corruption of the Greek legends on the coins of these Parthian kings, is consistent with the notion, that they followed, instead of preceding, the Kaḍphises dynasty; we incline, therefore, to assign to them a date, in the middle of the first century of our era, between the Kadphises, and Kanerki races of kings.

For the reasons thus stated, we suppose, that during the ascendancy of the Kadphises' kings, the Greco-Parthian party was not extinguished, but, holding out in various free cities, and communities, made terms of submission, abiding their time to re-assert their independence, and that they found that time, in the middle of the first century of our era. From coins, we have the following kings of kings for this period, and their assumption of the lofty title of the Parthian king, shows that their dominion must for the time have been extensive.

A. D. 40. UNDOPHERRES, whom first we find calling himself ΒΑΣΙΛΕΩΣ ΣΤΗΡΟΣ, in imitation of the Hercules type coins of Hermæus, and of Korso Kadphises, (See plate IV., Nos. 8, 9, 10, and 11,) and afterwards ΒΑΣΙΛΕΩΣ ΒΑΣΙΛΕΩΝ ΜΕΓΑΛΟΥ, (See plate VIII. Nos. 6 and 7,) Arian, *Maharajasa Raja-rajasa Tradatasa Mahatasa Pharahitasa.** The change of titles seems clearly to mark this king, as the founder of his race and dynasty, and he seems to have retained the title of Saviour in his Arian legend, after dropping it in the Greek.

A.D. 55. GONDOPHERRES, or GONDOPHARES, who also called himself king of kings, *Maharaja* and *Raja-raja*, and took the same Arian name of Pharahitasa. (See plate VIII. No. 9.)

A. D. 70. ABAGASUS, king of kings. Arian *Abakhafasa.* This name is, by Professor Lassen, supposed to be identical with Vologeses : but the supposition is built on the idea, that these Ario-Parthian coins were, of necessity, coins of Parthian kings, whereas it seems much more rational to ascribe them to Parthians, who established for themselves a separate and independent sovereignty in Kâbool, and the Parapamisus.

A. D. 80. ABALGASIUS. The Greek legends of these

* Captain Cunningham reads the name *Undopharasa.*

coins, (Nos. 11 and 12, plate VIII.) are so corrupt, as to be scarcely decypherable. The name, however, is legible, and Captain Cunningham, who published the coins in the Asiatic Journal of Calcutta, made out the Arian legend to be, "*Maharajasa tradatasa Abagasasa Andophara Khudra putrasa.*" "Of the saviour king Abagasus, younger son of Undopherres."

Pakores, king of kings, whose coin,* with bilinqual Greek and Arian legend, was found by Colonel Stacey, in Kandahar, we do not suppose to be of the Undopherres dynasty, the head, and general style, being so very different. The coin may belong to the brother of Vologeses, successor to Gotarzes, for Josephus tells us, that, on this king's first accession, he made over the province of Media (which of course would include Khorasân, and as much of Ariana as belonged at the time to Parthia,) to his younger brother Pakores, and Armenia to another brother Tiridates. There is no reason whatever to suppose that this Pakores had sovereignty in Kâbool, or on the Indus, and he seems not to have held power long, for the general sovereignty of Vologeses was very soon re-established over the entire Parthian dominions.

The above Ario-parthian supposed dynasty brings down the history of Kâbool, and the Punjâb, to the close of the first century of our era, when we find

* See Fig. 13, Plate, No. VIII.

a new race of Scythian kings, issuing gold, and copper money, of quite a different device, and style, from any before current. These bear the name of Kanerkes, at first with the title of ΒΑΣΙΛΕΥΣ ΒΑΣΙΛΕΩΝ, in the nominative, and the king's name ΚΑΝΗΡΚΟΥ in the genitive, (See Nos. 12 and 14, plate VIII.) but afterwards, with the Indian title of Rao Nano Rao substituted, and the number, and varieties of the Kanerki coins, betoken a long dominion for kings of the race.

The great peculiarities of this coinage are, first, that no coin of the Kanerkis has yet been found bilingual: on all, the only characters are Greek, but these become at last so corrupt, as to be quite illegible. Secondly, The king standing, or in bust to the waist, is given always on the obverse, in a Tartar or Indian dress, with the name and titles in a Greek legend round, while on the reverse we have Mithraic representations of the Sun, or Moon, with ΗΛΙΟΣ, ΝΑΝΑΙΑ, ΟΚΡΟ, ΜΙΟΡΟ, ΜΑΟ, ΑΘΡΟ, or some other mystical name of these luminaries, also in Greek letters: and, Thirdly, upon all the coins of Kanerki kings, the same monogram is found, as was used by the Kadphises dynasty, after assuming the title of "king of kings," being borrowed apparently from the nameless Soter Megas. This would seem to indicate, that the Kanerki dynasty, though interrupted as we suppose by the intervention of Ario-Parthians, was yet a continuance of the same tribe and nation, as its predecessors of the name of Kadphises. A very few of the

Kanerki coins have been found, with the Siva and Bull device on the reverse, the bull's head being to the left, instead of, as in the coins of Kadphises, to the right. This seems to indicate, that the Hindoo religion was not wholly discountenanced, and rejected. But the Mithraic worship so much predominates, that we are compelled to look upon this latter as the state religion of the Kanerkis, whence derived is still matter for learned discussion and controversy.*

The Kanerki, and Oerki, coins are not sufficiently distinct, to enable us to give, seriatim, a list or catalogue of the different sovereigns. Their power must have continued for more than two centuries, for we find, in the topes that have been opened, Kanerki coins, along with those of Kadphises, and other predecessors of the race, mixed with coins of the Sassanian kings of the third and fourth century of our era. During the entire period of the sovereignty of this race, Greek, corrupt doubtless to the last degree, but still recognisable as Greek, and no other character, is found upon any of its coins. The use of this character does not seem to have ceased with the Kanerkis, for we find the same continued, with a sovereign represented as riding upon an elephant, and called, so far as the name and title can be decyphered, *Rao nana*

* Nanaia is traced to Armenia: In plate V., fig. 7, we give after Wilson, the earliest numismatic evidence of the name and worship. The name round the bust of the obverse is so far lost, that we discover only that it begins with D. and ends with BISES, which shows it to be Persian.

Rao Kenorano. See plate IX., No. 13, and plate XII., 10 to 15.

After this, the Greek characters yielded to Sanscrit, and we give two of the plates prepared by Mr. James Prinsep, purposely to show, how the style and device, of the gold coinage especially, both of Kadphises, and the Kanerkis, was carried on till it grew more and more corrupt, and was at last entirely lost, through the deterioration of art, under the princes of Hindoo race, who succeeded to the more energetic Greeks and Scythians.

Professor Wilson has added to his work notices of the Sassanian, and of Hindoo, and early Mahomedan coins, found in Afghanistan and Upper India. These form a separate subject, with which at present we have nothing to do; but before concluding, we would offer a few more observations regarding the language found upon the new coins, which we have called Arian, and not Bactrian, because there is no evidence of its being the language of the countries watered by the Oxus and Jaxartes.

Although the Greek characters outlived the Arian, upon the money of the Punjâb, and of the Kâbool valley, we have proof in the Arian inscriptions, found on the stones and relics of topes in both regions, that Arian only was the written language of general use, when Greek was quite extinct.

This language was adopted, first by the Greek kings, from Eucratides down to Hermæus, it was then taken up by the Scythians, who crossed the Paropamisus, Imaus, or Hindoo Koosh, and also by Parthians, who asserted their independence in Afghanistan: we conclude, therefore, it must have been the vernacular language of the Paropamisan range, of Kâbool, and perhaps of Herât, and Kandahar; we find it also in the topes of Manikyala in the Punjâb. Now the first thing to be observed of the language is, that, unlike both Greek and Sanscrit, it is written semitically from right to left. But while the art of writing was in its infancy, and each character had a separate and distinct form, never joined into a running hand, it mattered little whether the characters were placed in one order, or in the other. We know that the earliest Greek was written alternately, as a plough is driven, and the tombs of Tuscan kings, recently opened in Italy, contain inscriptions in Greek characters, written like the Arian from right to left. The Mongolians, also, who adopted the Syrian alphabet, write it in lines downwards like the Chinese: consequently, as the Arian written characters are always found with the letters disjoined, in a primitive form, we are not disposed, on account of the order of arrangement, to conclude that the language has a semitic origin, or any close affinity with the languages of that class. We find, on the contrary, that all the Arian words yet read, which represent epithets, or titles, such as the words for "king," for "saviour," for "just," "illustrious," "unconquered," "victorious," &c. are pure Sanscrit, meaning the same thing precisely in that language.

For ΒΑΣΙΛΕΩΣ	we have	*Maharajasa.*
ΜΕΓΑΛΟΥ		*Mahatasa.*
ΒΑΣΙΛΕΩΣ ΒΑΣΙΛΕΩΝ		*Rajadirajasa.*
ΔΙΚΑΙΟΥ		*Dhamikasa.*
ΝΙΚΗΦΟΡΟΥ		*Jyadharasa.*
ΕΠΙΦΑΝΟΥΣ		*Tejamasa.*
ΑΝΙΚΗΤΟΥ		*Apatihatasa.*
For Son		*Putasa, &c. &c.**

This is evidence of very close affinity with Sanscrit, and leads to the hope that by a further use of the coins, as a key for settling the alphabet, the dialects of Sanscrit, and the Pooshtoo especially, may be applied, to the complete decyphering, and translation of the inscriptions in Arian characters, which have been found on the relics in topes, and on rocks, and other remains of the period of its use. Fac-similes of several of these inscriptions have been made, and are now in the hands of Professor Lassen, from whose learning and ingenuity we hope the best result. We know that this work occupied the latest attention of Mr. James Prinsep, who was confident, that through the coins, the language being ascertained to be of Sanscrit origin, a sufficient clue existed for the complete development of the antiquarian treasures locked up in the inscriptions; indeed, that he considered himself to have already mastered the first difficulties of decyphering them, and to be in progress towards the full ascertainment of the meaning of one at least, if not of two of these inscriptions.

* See Plate XIII. for the forms of letters.

The work he left incomplete, remains to be accomplished by those who continue to feel interest, and to give attention to these researches, and we look to Professor Lassen, in particular, for an early solution through these inscriptions, of the problems, he has himself so largely raised, in respect to the history and antiquities of the Paropamisan regions.

A further remark we have to make in respect to this Arian language, is, that it seems to have superseded the ancient Sanscrit of the days of Asoka, which was adopted by Agathocles and Pantaleon, the first of whom we know, from the pure Greek style of his other coins, to be one of the earliest of the Grecian kings. If these two kings had not found the Sanscrit language in use, they would scarcely have placed it on their coins. After them, however, the Sanscrit characters were entirely disused. Menander, the known Indian conqueror, never seems to have adopted, or at least to have coined with, the language of Asoka: from which circumstance we infer, that the characters on the coins of Agathocles and Pantaleon were not vernacular, but had been introduced by the Indian sovereigns, who, following the first Chandra Goopta, retained dominion over the provinces ceded by the first Seleucus, until they were restored by Asoka to the Great Antiochus. This hypothesis only will explain, both the adoption of Sanscrit by the governors left by Antiochus in those provinces, and the early discontinuance of the character.

Again, Arian characters only are found on the

vases, relics, and stones, discovered on excavating the tumuli, or topes, as well of the Punjâb, as of Jelâlabad, and Kâbool. This seems to prove, that at the time of the erection of these topes, the Arian was not only the vernacular language of the districts where they stand, but the language also of the priests, and people concerned in preparing the vases, and articles used in the funeral obsequies of the great. If Brahman priests or Boodhist Sramanas had been employed, they assuredly would have used the characters, and language of India, viz. those of the coins of Agathocles, and Pantaleon, already once before introduced into these regions. Scythian priests, again, would have brought the forms of writing, in use beyond the Jaxartes, and Belout Tag mountains. And, as Greek was always, so long as it lasted, the more honored language, being that found on the obverse of the coins, it is difficult to understand, why the same language should not have been used, in preference to the Arian, for inscriptions on the funeral paraphernalia. All these are questions, which the decyphering of a few of the inscriptions will set for ever at rest.

In the hope of drawing more general attention to them, and perhaps of eliciting a successful display of ingenuity, in quarters, where the material, upon which to exercise it, might otherwise be wanting, we give in two separate plates,* transcripts of two Arian inscriptions, taken with great care, for

* Plates XVI. and XVII.

submission to the late Mr. James Prinsep. These are the inscriptions referred to in the last paper he wrote upon Bactrian relics, which was published in the Journal of the Asiatic Society, for July, 1838. In his note book, is an analysis of one of them, and tentative readings of both, which we also submit to help the student, who may devote himself to the task of decyphering them. We have only one wish—to see the end attained, to see extracted from these inscriptions, some undeniable evidence, in support, or confutation of the conjectures, we have here put together; and so to obtain for all time, a record of facts and circumstances, that may be added confidently to the historical remains, of ages and of regions, which for many reasons are objects of interest, and of increasing curiosity.

In order that nothing may be wanting to those who undertake the decyphering of these inscriptions, we have judged it right, before bringing these pages to a conclusion, to reprint, from the Journal of the Asiatic Society of Calcutta, the substance of General Court's report of his finding that of Manikyala, which is evidently the fullest, and most important, in one of the topes or tumuli he there opened. We add also, an account, with drawings, of the relics, previously obtained by General Ventura in the larger tope, he had opened some time before in the same vicinity, upon which also there are inscriptions in the same Arian characters. The possession of the copper plates of these latter, prepared by Mr. James Prinsep for his Journal, enables us to give the whole complete. But we have to point out, that when first these relics came to hand, the Arian characters were quite unknown. They had not then been ascertained, and decyphered, by means of the bilingual Greek and Arian coins. It hence happened, that in the plate of General Ventura's relics, published in the Journal, the Arian inscriptions were given with the wrong side uppermost. Those obtained from Mr. Masson, having been so forwarded, led to the others also being similarly transcribed. In the present plate we have corrected this error.

The following is an abstract of General Court's description of Manikyala, and of his examination of the topes there.

Manikyala is the name of a small village situated on the high road from Attok to Lahore, a little more than half-way between the place first named, and the city of Jhilum. It is built on the ruins of a very ancient city of unknown origin; but the geographical position of the ruins, and particularly the abundance of coins found in them, affords the presumption that this city must have been the capital of all the country between the Indus and Hydaspes, a country which the ancients knew by the name of Taxila, and of which frequent mention is made in the history of Alexander.

There is at Manikyala a vast and massive cupola of great antiquity. It is visible at a considerable distance, having a height of about 80 feet, with a circumference of 310 or 320 feet. It is solidly built of quarried stones with lime cement. The outer layer is of sandstone. In the interior, the masonry is of granite and sandstone, mixed with a porous limestone. The outer surface is now so worn and furrowed, that it is not difficult to climb to the summit, which, when the building was new, must have been impossible. The architecture is simple; the only ornament is a range of small columns near the base, having ram's heads for their capitals, which, however, are now scarcely distinguishable. This is the tope opened by General Ventura.

Monuments of the same kind are met with at Rawul Pindi (in the Punjâb), in the Huzâra country west of Kâbool, at Jelâlabad (many of which have since been opened by Mr. Masson, and the relics of which are reported in Professor Wilson's Ariana Antiqua), also at Lagman, Kâbool, and Bâmean, and in the Khybur Pass.

Amongst the ruins of Manikyala, are fifteen other cupolas, smaller than that above described. These were all opened by General Court, and one in particular, distant about a cannon-shot to the N. N. E. of the present village, afforded rich materials. Amongst the coins, were some genuine Roman pieces,* and the stone which *served as a covering to the niche, which contained the relics, was*

* See Journal of Asiatic Society, for November, 1834, for plates of these Roman coins, which are of the first Cæsars, and of the Triumvirate.

found sculptured all over with inscriptions. It is from a wax impression of these inscriptions, that the annexed lithographic plate was prepared carefully by the late Mr. James Prinsep.

The cupola of the tope, which contained these relics, was so dilapidated, as almost to have escaped notice. Its height originally may have been 60 or 70 feet. It was pierced by General Court, from the centre of the summit, with a hole of about 20 feet diameter. The materials were a coarse concrete, very porous. The first discovery was of four copper coins, three feet only from the upper surface, one is of Kadphises, the other three of Kanerkes. Below this were large blocks, which made it difficult to penetrate the masonry. On working ten feet through these, a rectangular cell was found, built with dressed stones firmly united with mortar. The cell was in the form of a paralellogram, having its four sides corresponding with the four cardinal points, and at the top was one massive slab, upon which were the inscriptions. In the centre of the cell stood a copper urn, round which were placed symmetrically, eight medals of copper, much corroded, but with sufficient left of the stamp and device, to show two to be of the Kadphises type, and the rest Kanerkis. The urn was carefully enveloped in a wrapper of white linen, adhering tightly, but which fell to shreds when the urn was handled. In the copper urn was a smaller silver one, the space being filled with an earthy paste impregnated with verdigris and still moist; there was found in this pasty substance, a thread, or string, tied in a knot, which also, on being handled, was reduced to powder. The silver of this interior vase was quite corroded, so as to break into pieces.* Within it was a much smaller vessel of gold, bedded in the same brown paste, along with seven silver coins, all evidently Roman. The gold vessel contained four small gold coins of Greco-Scythian type, all Kanerkis, and two precious stones, with four decayed pearls bored as for ear-rings.

The discovery of the inscription led to a re-examination of the opening, made by General Ventura in the large tope at the same place, but no stone could be found there with any trace of letters, nor were inscriptions found in other topes opened at Manikyala by General Court.

General Ventura's operations for opening the large tope, were commenced on the 27th of April, 1830, at the bottom of the cupola on the south side, but, finding there nothing but rubbish, he recommenced from the summit. At the depth of three feet, he met with six coins, and after penetrating to twelve feet, the building was of solid large quarried stones, through which the work was carried on with difficulty. On reaching ten feet below the surface of this masonry, another coin was found in a clod of earth, and at the depth of twenty feet, one

* The General probably mistook lead, or tin, for silver, for the corrosion of silver, when the copper was nearly perfect, is scarcely intelligible.

silver and six copper coins.* Two days afterwards the workmen reached a box of iron or copper, which was broken by their pickaxes, and contained a small box of pure gold, (Fig. 1. Plate XIV.) in the centre of which was an opal. The box contained a gold coin, weighing 122 grains, of the Kanerki race, the Greek very corrupt, (Fig. 2. Plate XIV.) also a gold seal-ring set with a sapphire, having a Pahlavee inscription, (Fig. 3. Plate XIV.) a small bit of ruby (Balas or Budukshany), three small silver coins without stamp, a Sassanian silver coin, (Fig. 8. Plate XIV.) of a type corresponding with that assigned by Longperier to king Sarbaraz, who reigned only forty days, and on the margin of which both he and Professor Wilson read the Mahommedan Bismillah. Mr. James Prinsep considered this to be a coin of Sapor II. because of the crescent and wings at the top of the crown, or head dress, but the subject was not then so well understood as at present. There were also found, two other Sassanian coins, of types not given in Longperier, but having Deva-nagri legends, (Nos. 10, 11. Plate XIV.) From a more perfect specimen of No. 11, obtained through Sir A. Burnes, its Deva-nagri legend was read by Mr. James Prinsep thus—*Sri hitivira Airan cha parameswara sri Vahitigan deva-*

* General Ventura unfortunately mixed these coins, so as to be unable afterwards to discriminate, which were found at each of these different depths, but all were apparently of the same age as the Sassanian coins, that is as late as the fifth century.

janita. A rude silver coin of India, corrupted from the Kanerki type, and evidencing a very modern date for this deposit, completed the list of articles belonging to it.

Not satisfied with the discovery thus made, General Ventura proceeded with the perforation, until on the 25th of May it had been carried to the depth of forty-five feet. There on lifting a large quarried stone, a similar was found below, with a hole excavated in its centre, wherein was deposited a copper box, (Fig. 12. Plate XIV.) with the lid decayed, and having inside a piece of cloth, (Fig. 13), a chrystal drop, (Fig. 14), and a small cylinder of pure gold (Fig. 15.) Carrying the excavation yet further, a copper coin was found at the depth of fifty-four feet, and three more Sassanian coins, with some trifling articles, all much corroded.

On the last day of May, at the depth of sixty-four feet, an immense slab was reached, which laid open a chamber, built up with stone and cement. In this was a box of copper, (Fig. 19. Plate XV.) filled with a brown liquid substance, which upon analysis was found to contain decomposed animal substance. Inside of this, was a turned brass box, well preserved, and showing still the marks of the turning tool, but with the top broken off; on the lid of the box was an Arian inscription, punctured circularly as shown in Fig. 20. Plate XV. In the brass box, were five copper coins of the Kanerki, and Kenorano type (Figs. 28 to 32), and a cylinder of pure gold, all bedded in the liquid brown substance above mentioned. The cylinder opened with a lid fitting inwards, and contained some fragments of amber, or glass, and a small piece of string, (Fig. 23. Plate XV.) together with a small gold coin (Fig. 24. Plate XV.) weighing thirty grains, (a semi-drachma), of the type Kanerki Koranos, also a plain disc of silver, bearing two lines of Arian characters deeply cut, (Fig. 26. Plate XV.) A small piece of gold, (Fig. 25. Plate XV.) complete the list of these relics, all which were presented by General Ventura to Mr. James Prinsep, and now form part of the cabinet belonging to his estate.

General Ventura carried the excavation afterwards to the foundation below the masonry, but found nothing more: we have, therefore, in the above relics, the first and most ancient deposit of this tope. The coins forbid our ascribing it to a period earlier than the reign of Kenorano, the latest of the Kanerkis, if he was at all of that race: We find, however, that while the coins have still the Greek legends, the inscriptions on all the relics are exclusively Arian. This is the case as well in this tope, as in that afterwards opened by General Court.

It is probable that General Court's was the more ancient of the two, for in that we find Roman coins mixed with those of Kanerki and Kadphises, but none of Kenorano, the Elephant mounted king, and none Sassanian. In both, however, the inscriptions are all in the same character: and, with this statement of the circumstances attending their discovery, we commit them again to the ingenuity and research of the learned. They have already been published, with the same plates, in the pages of the Journal of the Asiatic Society of Calcutta.

Mr. Masson, excited by the interest evinced regarding the relics obtained from the topes of Manikyala, opened as we have before stated, very many at Daranta, and Hidda, near Jelâlabad, and in other parts of the Kâbool valley. The particulars of his discoveries will be found given at length, in Professor Wilson's Ariana Antiqua, to which we refer our readers. Two inscriptions, however, found on a cylinder extracted by Mr. Masson, from a tope at Jelâlabad, are given in Plate XV., as published originally in Calcutta, along with the Manikyala relics. They were forwarded by this gentleman to Calcutta in 1834, with the first notice of his discoveries in this branch of archæology. Our repetition of the publication will not, therefore, we feel assured, be regarded as an usurpation of his right in them; but it is proper to make the acknowledgment, that these are a part of his labours, and as such will be found also in the pages of Professor Wilson.

One thing seems to be proved by these late searches into the interior of the topes or tumuli of the Punjâb and Kâbool valley; namely, that they are sepulchral monuments, erected for the deposit and preservation of the urns, in which the ashes, and unconsumed remains of persons of distinction were collected, after burning their bodies on the funeral pile. Arrian expressly tells us that it was not the custom in India to erect expensive tombs to kings; but we know that eight stupas, or topes, nearly similar in form to these, were erected over the remains of Sakhya Boodh, after his body had been burnt in Behar. The inscription on the slab, which closed the chamber of the tope, opened by General Court, contains letters, which are unmistakeably "*Maharajasa,*" being identical with those letters on the bilingual coins. That tope, therefore, must have contained the remains of a king, and we infer, that he was a king of the Kanerki race, from the coins of this type being the latest found in them. But it is singular, that the gold coins found in the interior cylinder, have neither the title of Maharaja, nor its Greek equivalent ΒΑΣΙΛΕΥΣ, Rao nano rao, being the words of their legend, which are supposed later titles. This adds to the curiosity that must be felt, to decypher, and settle the interpretation of the entire inscription, in which we recognise the earlier title. The coins and relics found at different depths, above the lower chamber in both topes, may, not improbably, be similar remains of members of the same family, who died while the topes were in course of erection, or not very long after their completion. The deposit of coins, made with each sepulchral urn, seems to be a custom derived from the Greeks, to provide the soul of the deceased with Charon's fee. But we have yet no evidence that the erection of topes was a practice of the Greek colonists, for, in no single tope yet opened, has there been any Greek inscription found, or coin of a Grecian king, or other relic referable to the known institutions of that race. The topes seem to be of Scythian origin, and are in all respects analogous to the mounds, and tumuli, left by invaders of the Scythian and Gothic race, in all parts of the world, overrun, or traversed by them. But it seems strange, that, while we know that the coins of Menander and Apollodotus formed the general currency of these regions, Roman coins should be sought out to be deposited with the inmost relics, to the exclusion of these.

Kupoordigiri, where the other Arian inscription referred to above was found, is a town in the midst of ruins, situated about forty miles N. E. from Peshawur. The inscription was on a large stone, from which a part had been broken off. Sir A. Burnes furnished, together with a copy made from sight, an impression taken from the stone itself with wet paper and lamp black. It is from these collated, that the copy was made, which has been found in Mr. James Prinsep's Note-book, and from which Plate XVII. is taken. On the plate of the Kupourdigiri inscription, we give an analysis of that of Manikyala, made by Mr. James Prinsep, and found also in his Note-book. From the same source, we give two tentative readings of both the Kupoordigiri, and Manikyala inscriptions. These were found imperfect, and cannot be considered as the final readings, which Mr. James Prinsep contemplated publishing with an interpretation, but was prevented executing, by the attack of paralysis, which terminated in his decease. We give them only as materials to help future labourers in the same field.

Tentative Readings of Kupoordigiri inscription, Plate XVII.

First—Parshitama ja ra ka dhi — rajasa
tee
Sataya sa tetáre sarke u chethiya,
bhu
—Tala karmma diga keta bhute fantesa tata yeta khsa
tin
Antiripale pidhi n varsa khatlesuram bha kata
Sha ra kiti vrija vadhi de ke riti di ya pade shu.

Second—Aparajita matava
Satadasa tituriso juke sidhi ja—
Jau a tra ta mmari da keta tiphira ti sa tuta ji tanha
Arati pala pitira va jusa ra te sa ra mu ka ta
Sata ki ti vuta vari de ke ritari jaupatâ.

Tentative Readings of part of Manikyala Inscription, Plate XVI.

First— gh? ba f
Keraladhara rusti sa anapa viha sati va
* 120
Sta CXX swan apurbeswa Maharajasa kane
Shsm
State vusta khata d — sa tatbakatala
sana
Vacha safa — ai sisa mudra pasa
Hâra i dwasa dasa apakha niti haja
Nana i biana — kestata dwi dra wuta.

— — — — —

* Qy. borrowed from the Romans?

Second—Pera ra na ra rudhi sa Afapa viaza ma va
— 220 vana putha ka Maharajasa kani
Ksha rashva shr Khuda ra cha o dadu ka lala
Va — yaphana — shisa mutra pasa
ja
Hata e rt sa dasa apakha pheti ha va
Tratra — anare —

The manuscript gives no more, and there is no attempt at translation.

FINIS.

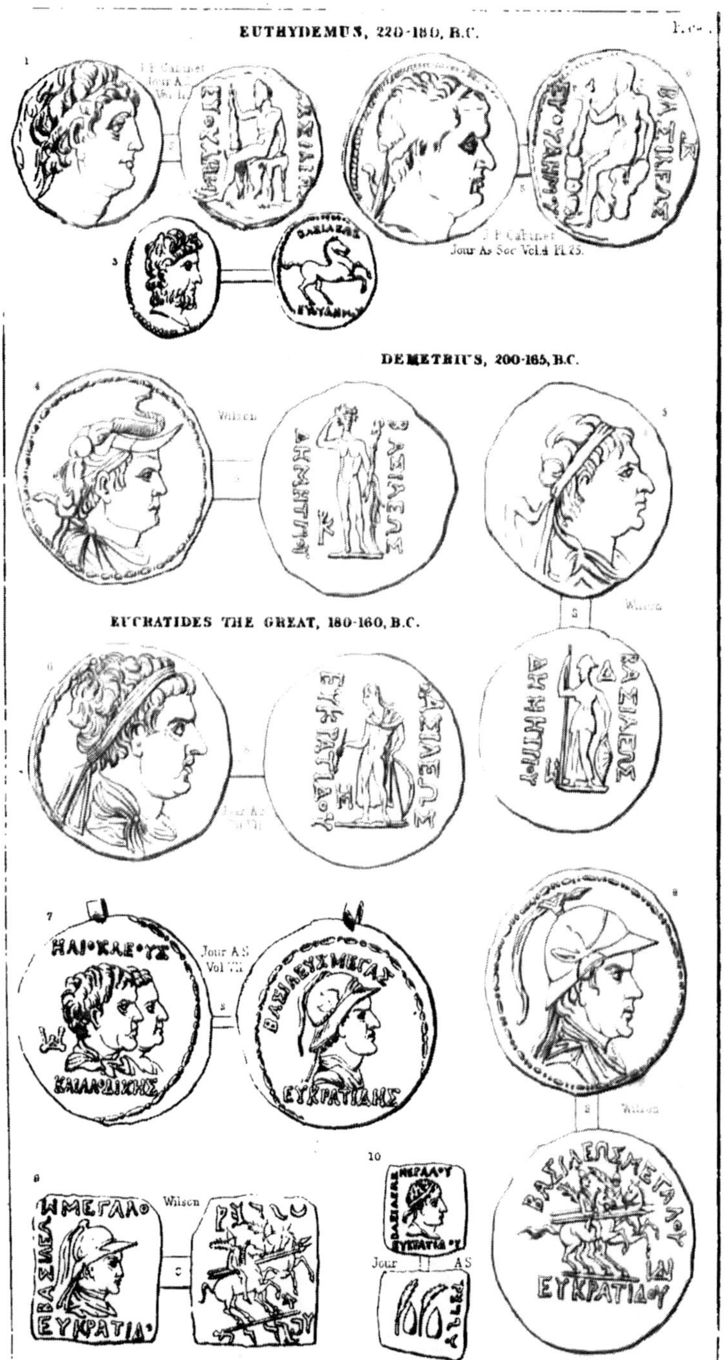
EUTHYDEMUS, 220-180, B.C.
Jour As Soc Vol.4 Pl.25
DEMETRIUS, 200-165, B.C.
Wilson
EUCRATIDES THE GREAT, 180-160, B.C.
Jour A.S Vol VII
ΒΑΣΙΛΕΥΣ ΜΕΓΑΣ
ΕΥΚΡΑΤΙΔΗΣ
ΕΥΚΡΑΤΙΔΟΥ
Wilson
Jour A.S

Plate II
AGATHOCLES, 180-170, B.C.
Greek & Sanscrit
Wilson
Jour A.S. Vol 4 Pl 25
PANTALEON 170-165, B.C.
Greek & Sanscrit
Wilson
HELIOCLES, 160-155, B.C.
Dikaius Greek only
Wilson
ANTIMACHUS, 155-150, B.C.
pure Greek
A Cunningham Jour A.S.
HELIOCLES bilingual
Jour A.S. Vol VII P 18
Ventura
ANTIMACHUS Nikephoros bilingual
ARCHELAUS Nikephoros
ANTIALKIDES Nikephoros 150, B.C.
J P Cal
PHILOXENUS Aniketos
AMYNTAS Nikator
LYSIAS.

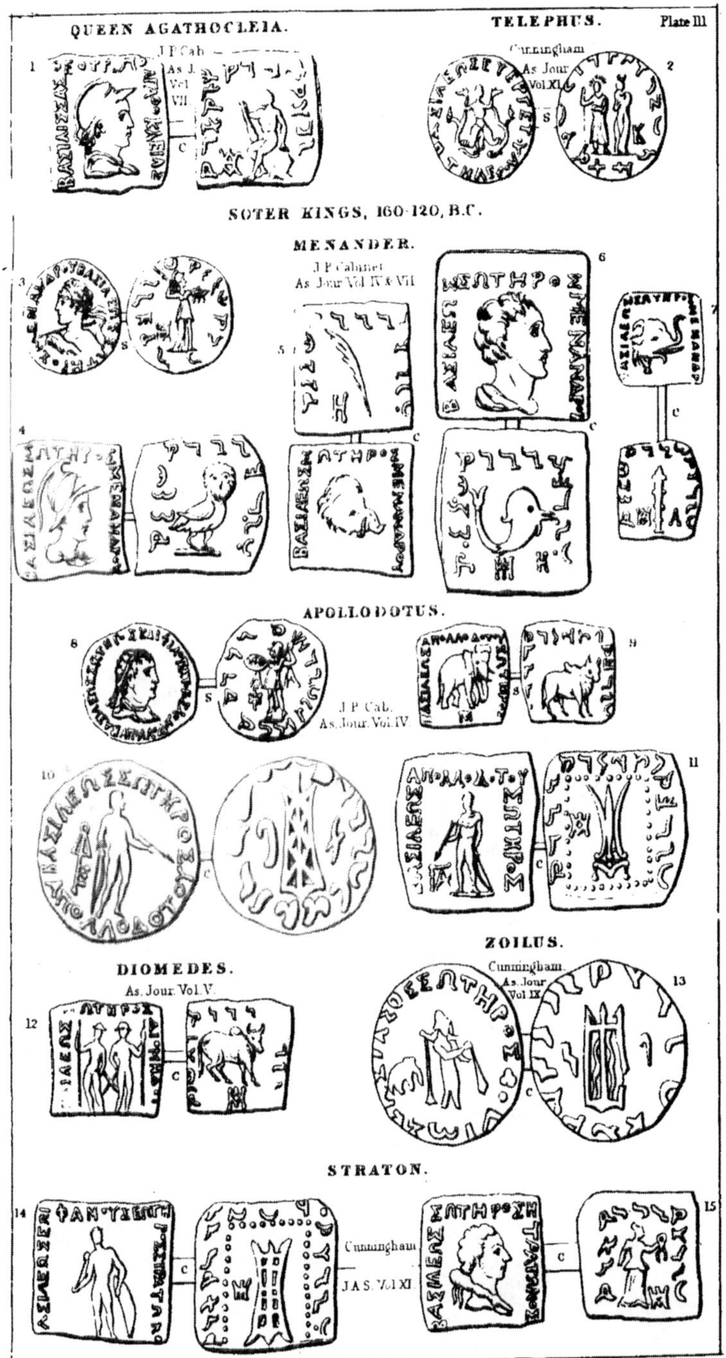
Plate III
QUEEN AGATHOCLEIA.
J.P.Cab.
As. J.
Vol.
VII.
TELEPHUS.
Cunningham
As. Jour.
Vol.XI.
SOTER KINGS, 160-120, B.C.
MENANDER.
J.P.Cabinet
As. Jour. Vol. IV & VII
APOLLODOTUS.
J.P.Cab.
As. Jour. Vol. IV.
DIOMEDES.
As. Jour. Vol. V.
ZOILUS.
Cunningham.
As. Jour.
Vol. IX.
STRATON.
Cunningham
J.A.S. Vol. XI.

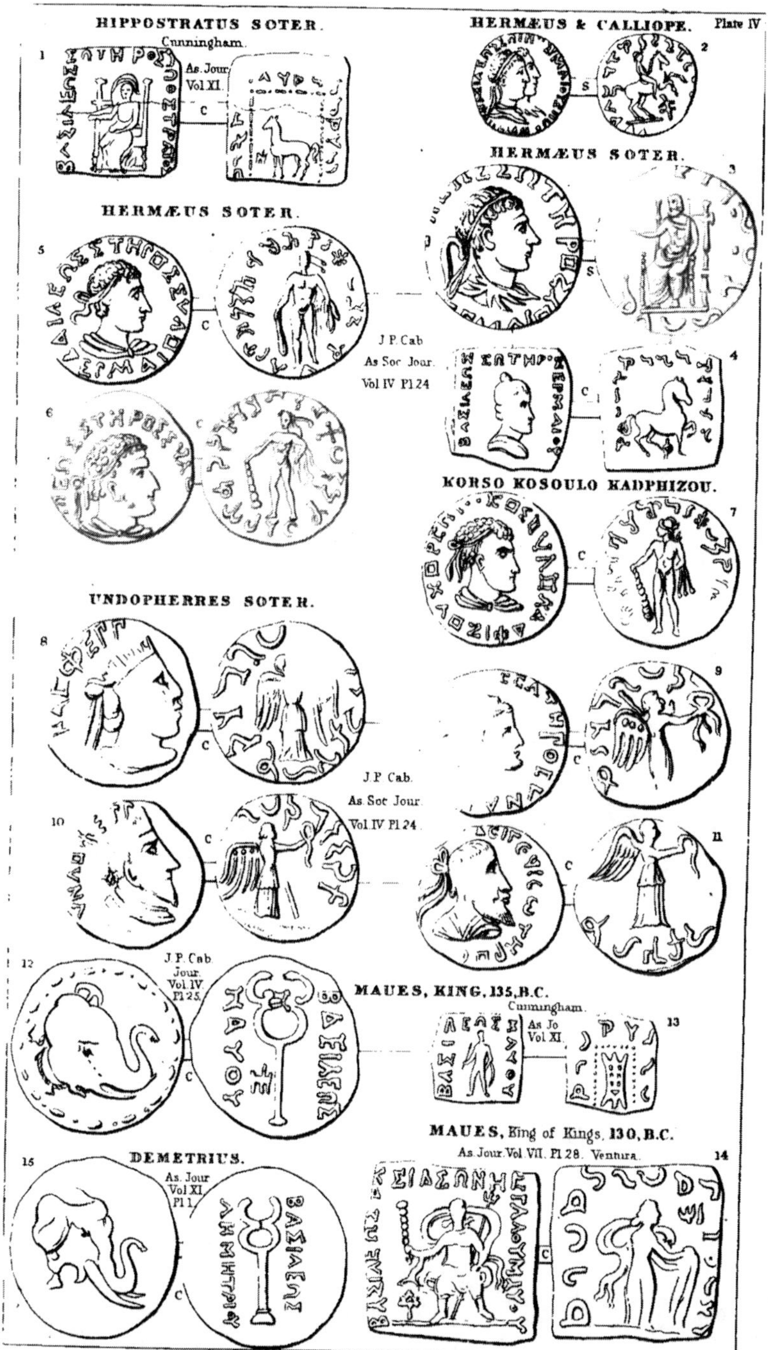
Plate IV
HIPPOSTRATUS SOTER.
Cunningham.
1
As. Jour. Vol XI.
HERMÆUS & CALLIOPE.
2
HERMÆUS SOTER.
3
HERMÆUS SOTER.
5
J.P. Cab
As Soc Jour.
Vol IV Pl 24
4
6
KORSO KOSOULO KADPHIZOU.
7
UNDOPHERRES SOTER.
8
9
J.P. Cab.
As. Soc Jour.
Vol. IV Pl 24.
10
11
12
J.P. Cab
Jour.
Vol. IV.
Pl 25.
MAUES, KING, 135, B.C.
Cunningham.
As Jo Vol XI.
13
MAUES, King of Kings, 130, B.C.
As. Jour. Vol VII. Pl 28. Ventura.
14
15
DEMETRIUS.
As. Jour Vol XI. Pl 1.

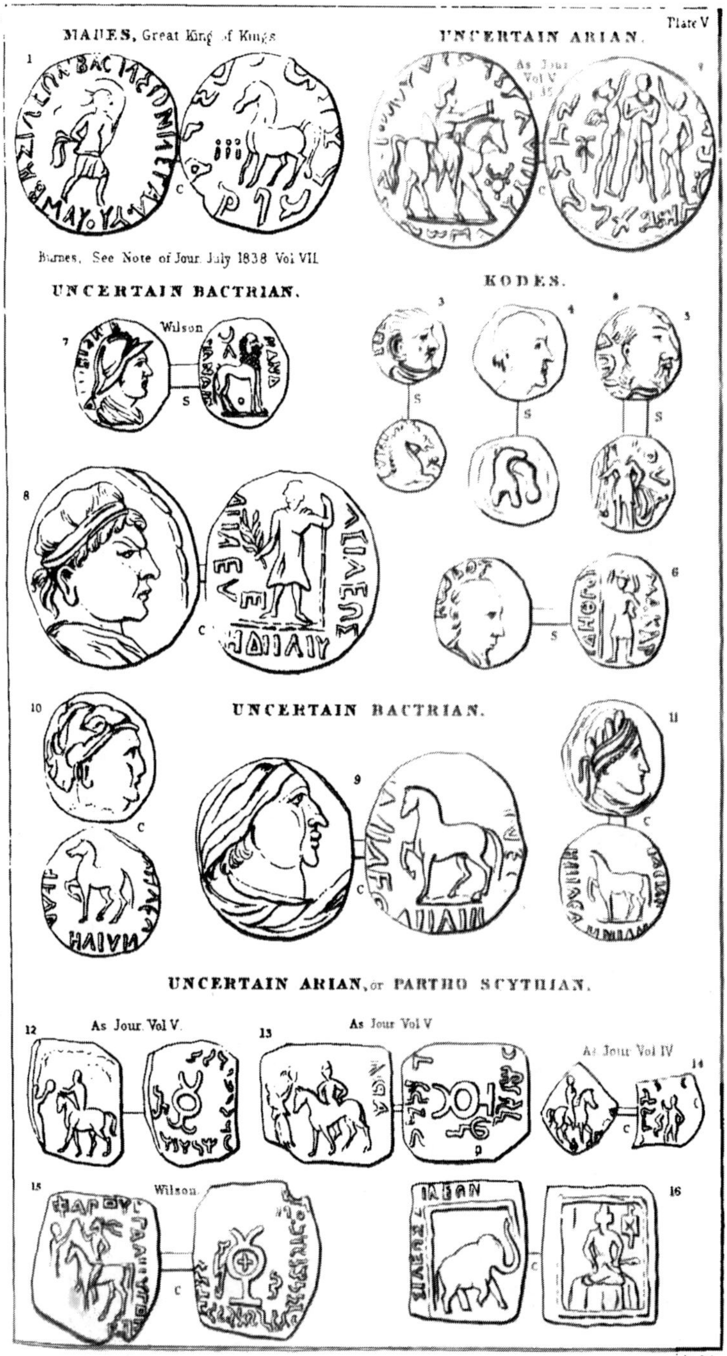
Plate V
MAUES, Great King of Kings
UNCERTAIN ARIAN.
Burnes, See Note of Jour. July 1838 Vol VII.
UNCERTAIN BACTRIAN.
KODES.
Wilson
UNCERTAIN BACTRIAN.
UNCERTAIN ARIAN, or PARTHO SCYTHIAN.
As Jour. Vol V.
As Jour. Vol V
As Jour. Vol IV
Wilson.

AZES, GREAT KING OF KINGS, 126, B.C. Plate VI

Plate VII

AZES, GREAT KING OF KINGS.

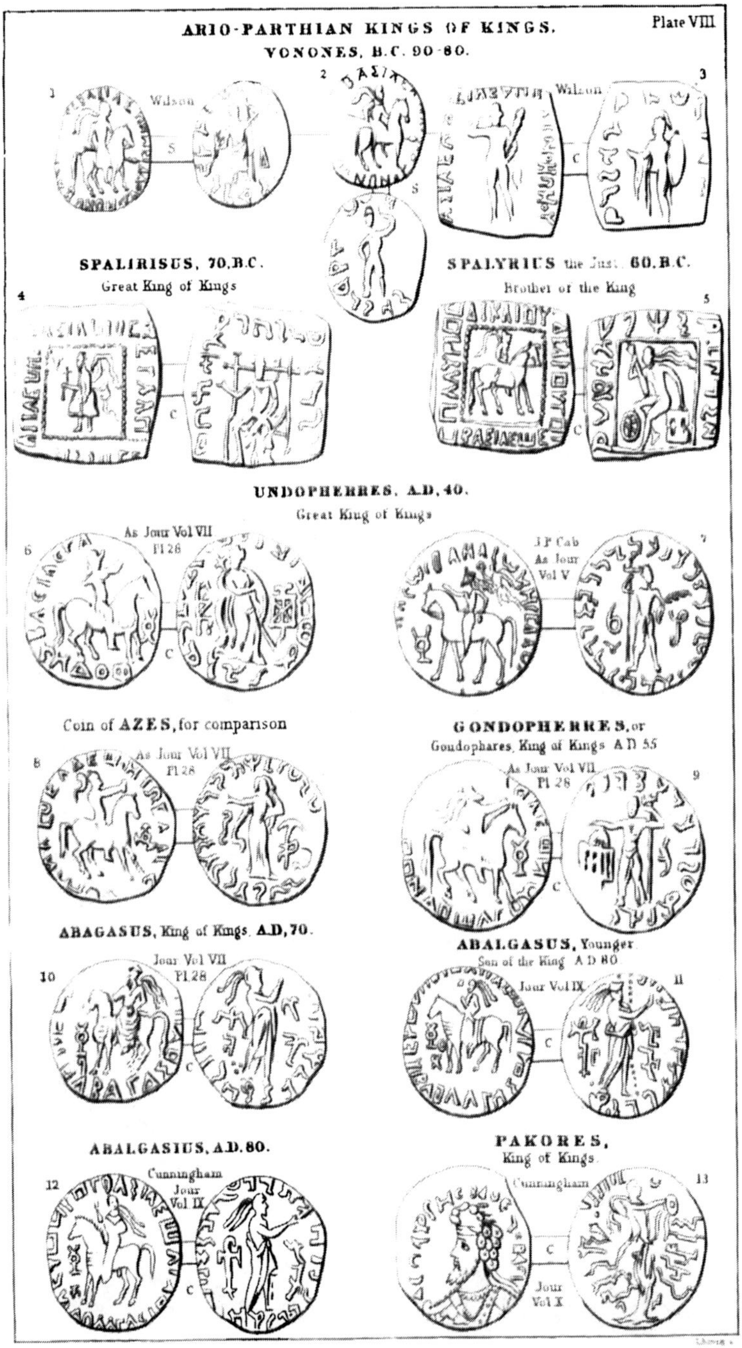
ARIO-PARTHIAN KINGS OF KINGS.
Plate VIII
VONONES, B.C. 90-80.
1
Wilson
S
2
S
3
Wilson
C
SPALIRISUS, 70, B.C.
Great King of Kings
4
C
SPALYRIUS the Just, 60, B.C.
Brother of the King
5
C
UNDOPHERRES, A.D, 40.
Great King of Kings
6
As Jour Vol VII
Pl 28
C
7
J P Cab
As Jour
Vol V
Coin of AZES, for comparison
8
As Jour Vol VII
Pl 28
GONDOPHERRES, or
Gondophares, King of Kings A D 55
As Jour Vol VII
Pl 28
9
C
ABAGASUS, King of Kings. A.D, 70.
10
Jour Vol VII
Pl 28
C
ABALGASUS, Younger
Son of the King A D 80
Jour Vol IX
11
C
ABALGASIUS, A.D. 80.
12
Cunningham
Jour
Vol IX
C
PAKORES,
King of Kings.
Cunningham
13
C
Jour
Vol X

SCYTHIAN & INDO-SCYTHIAN KINGS.
Plate IX
SOTER MEGAS,
J P Cab
KORANOS ZATHOS KADPHISES.
B.C. 10.
KADAPHES CHORANUS.
10, B.C.
KORSO KOZOULO KADPHISES.
OONM KADPHISES,
Great King of Kings A.D. 0
OOEMO KADPHISES,
Great King of Kings A.D. 0
KANERKES, King of Kings
A.D. 100.
KENO RANO RAO NANA RAO.
A.D. 200.
KANERKES, King of Kings
A.D. 100.

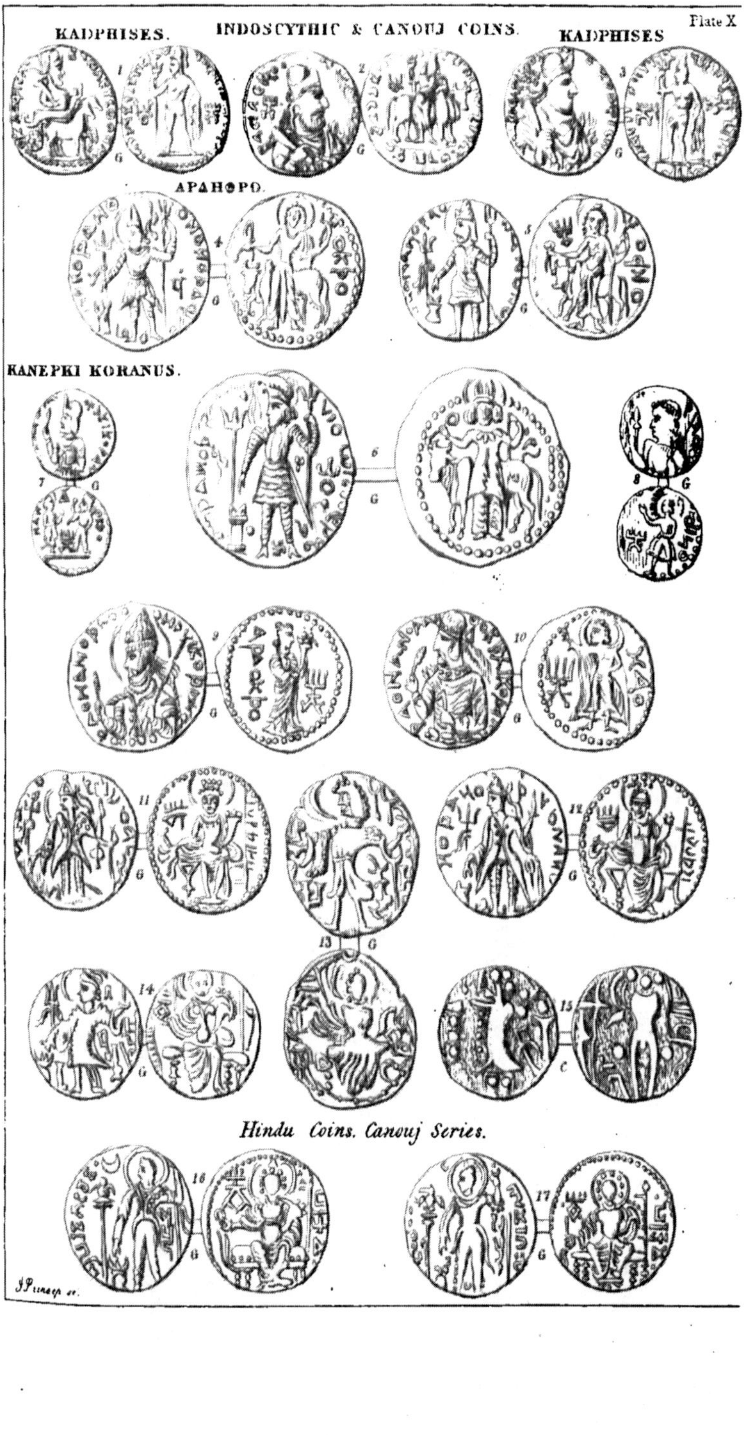
Plate X
INDOSCYTHIC & CANOUJ COINS.
KADPHISES.
KADPHISES
ΑΡΔΗΘΡΟ.
KANEPKI KORANUS.
Hindu Coins. Canouj Series.
J Prinsep sc.

MITHRAIC & HINDU COINS. Plate XI

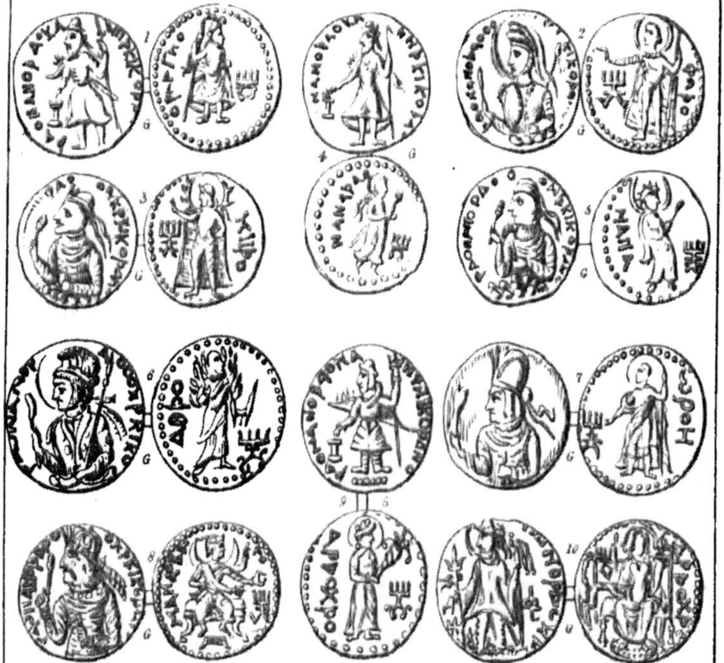

Hindu Coins. Canouj Series.
with Ardokro reverse.

INDOSCYTHIC COINS, KANERKOS GROUP.

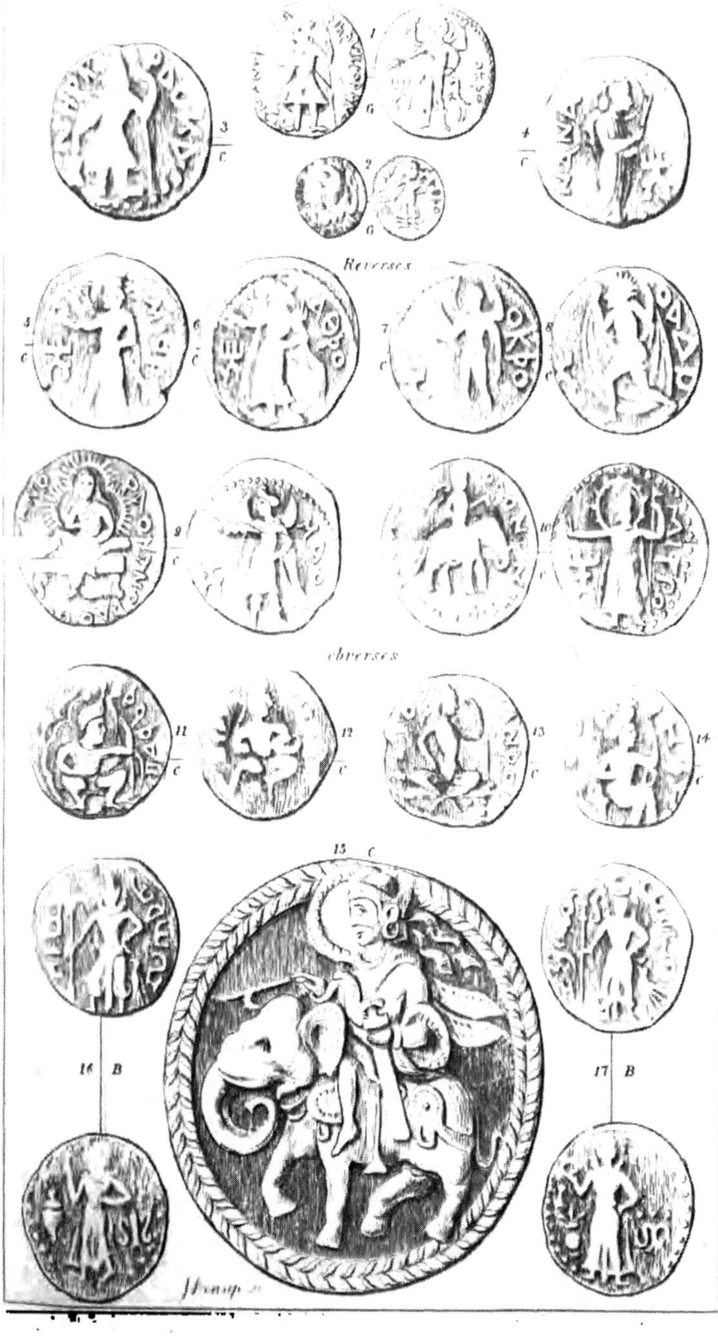

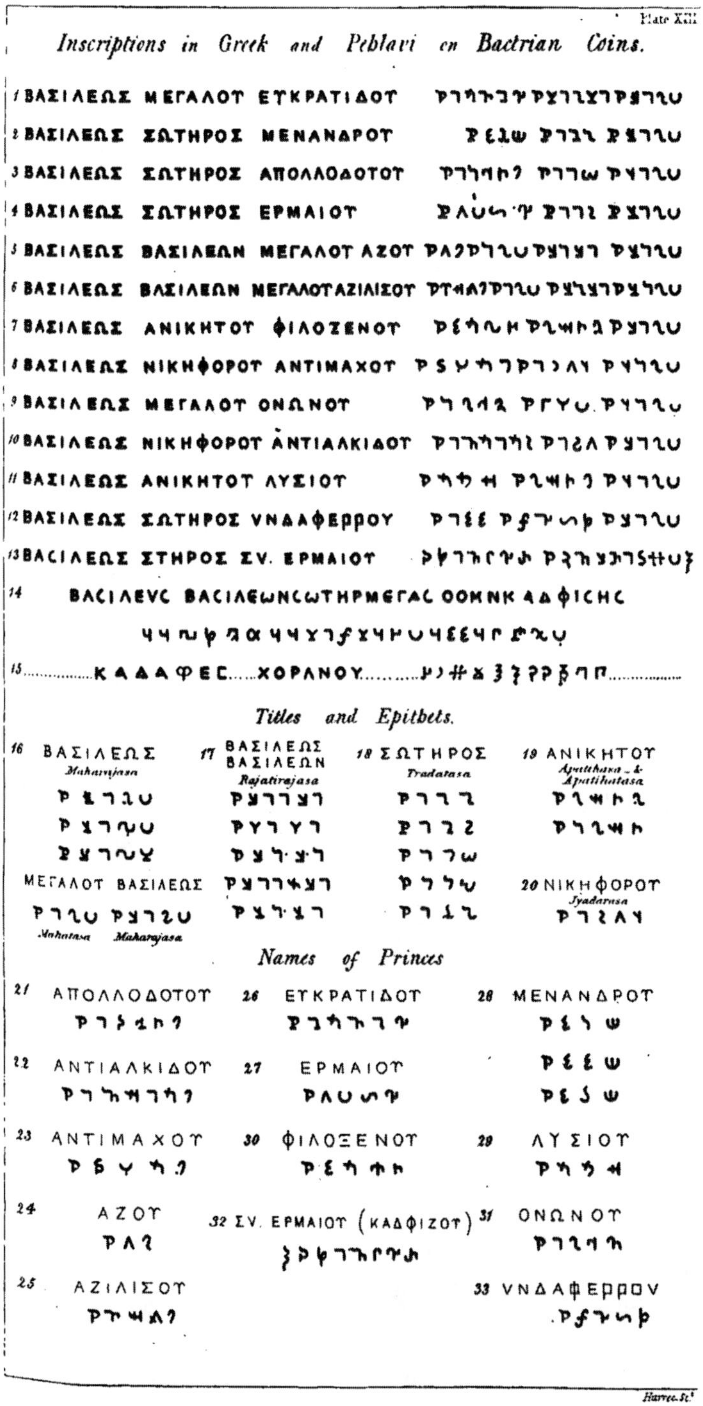
Plate XIII
Inscriptions in Greek and Pehlavi on Bactrian Coins.
1 ΒΑΣΙΛΕΩΣ ΜΕΓΑΛΟΥ ΕΥΚΡΑΤΙΔΟΥ
2 ΒΑΣΙΛΕΩΣ ΣΩΤΗΡΟΣ ΜΕΝΑΝΔΡΟΥ
3 ΒΑΣΙΛΕΩΣ ΣΩΤΗΡΟΣ ΑΠΟΛΛΟΔΟΤΟΥ
4 ΒΑΣΙΛΕΩΣ ΣΩΤΗΡΟΣ ΕΡΜΑΙΟΥ
5 ΒΑΣΙΛΕΩΣ ΒΑΣΙΛΕΩΝ ΜΕΓΑΛΟΥ ΑΖΟΥ
6 ΒΑΣΙΛΕΩΣ ΒΑΣΙΛΕΩΝ ΜΕΓΑΛΟΥ ΑΖΙΛΙΣΟΥ
7 ΒΑΣΙΛΕΩΣ ΑΝΙΚΗΤΟΥ ΦΙΛΟΞΕΝΟΥ
8 ΒΑΣΙΛΕΩΣ ΝΙΚΗΦΟΡΟΥ ΑΝΤΙΜΑΧΟΥ
9 ΒΑΣΙΛΕΩΣ ΜΕΓΑΛΟΥ ΟΝΩΝΟΥ
10 ΒΑΣΙΛΕΩΣ ΝΙΚΗΦΟΡΟΥ ΑΝΤΙΑΛΚΙΔΟΥ
11 ΒΑΣΙΛΕΩΣ ΑΝΙΚΗΤΟΥ ΛΥΣΙΟΥ
12 ΒΑΣΙΛΕΩΣ ΣΩΤΗΡΟΣ ΥΝΔΑΦΕΡΡΟΥ
13 ΒΑCΙΛΕΩΣ ΣΤΗΡΟΣ ΣΥ. ΕΡΜΑΙΟΥ
14 ΒΑCΙΛΕΥC ΒΑCΙΛΕΩΝ CΩΤΗΡ ΜΕΓΑC ΟΟΗΜΚ ΚΑΔΦΙCΗC
15 ΚΑΔΑΦΕC ΧΟΡΑΝΟΥ
Titles and Epithets.
16 ΒΑΣΙΛΕΩΣ Maharajasa
17 ΒΑΣΙΛΕΩΣ ΒΑΣΙΛΕΩΝ Rajatirajasa
18 ΣΩΤΗΡΟΣ Tradatasa
19 ΑΝΙΚΗΤΟΥ Apatihatasa
ΜΕΓΑΛΟΥ ΒΑΣΙΛΕΩΣ
Mahatasa Maharajasa
20 ΝΙΚΗΦΟΡΟΥ Jyadarasa
Names of Princes
21 ΑΠΟΛΛΟΔΟΤΟΥ
26 ΕΥΚΡΑΤΙΔΟΥ
28 ΜΕΝΑΝΔΡΟΥ
22 ΑΝΤΙΑΛΚΙΔΟΥ
27 ΕΡΜΑΙΟΥ
23 ΑΝΤΙΜΑΧΟΥ
30 ΦΙΛΟΞΕΝΟΥ
29 ΛΥΣΙΟΥ
24 ΑΖΟΥ
32 ΣΥ. ΕΡΜΑΙΟΥ (ΚΑΔΦΙΖΟΥ)
31 ΟΝΩΝΟΥ
25 ΑΖΙΛΙΣΟΥ
33 ΥΝΔΑΦΕΡΡΟΥ
Havree Sc.

Relics found in the Tope of Manikyala. Plate XIV

Plate XV
Relics found in the Tope of Manikyala.
Principal deposit
inscription on brass cylinder.
Characters scratched around a brass cylinder found in a Tope at Jelalabad.
ditto on the lid of the same.
J.Prinsep del et sculp.

FAC-SIMILE of A ARIAN INSCRIPTION FROM MAÑIKYALA TOPE.

¼th lin. dimensions

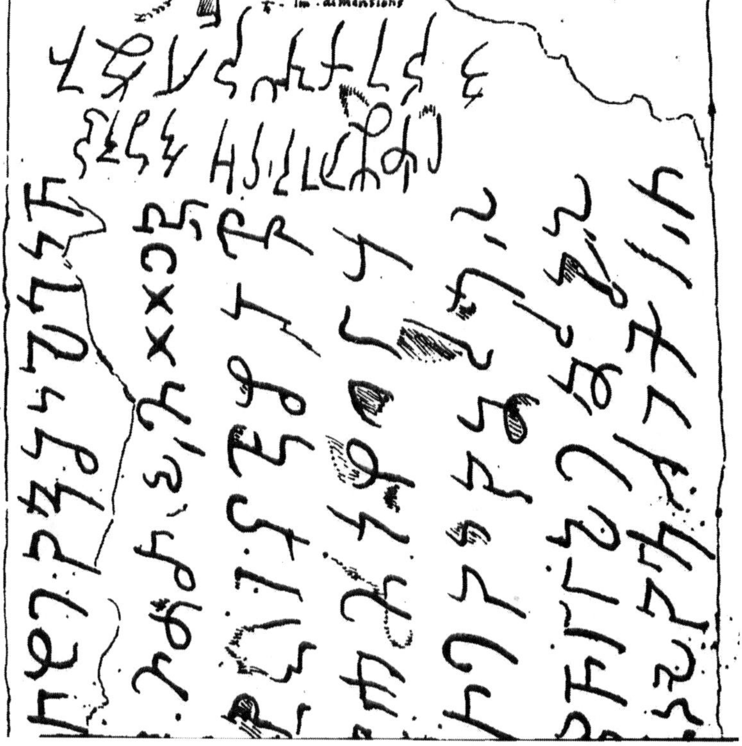

ANALYSIS of MANIKYALA INSCRIPTION by James PRINSEP.

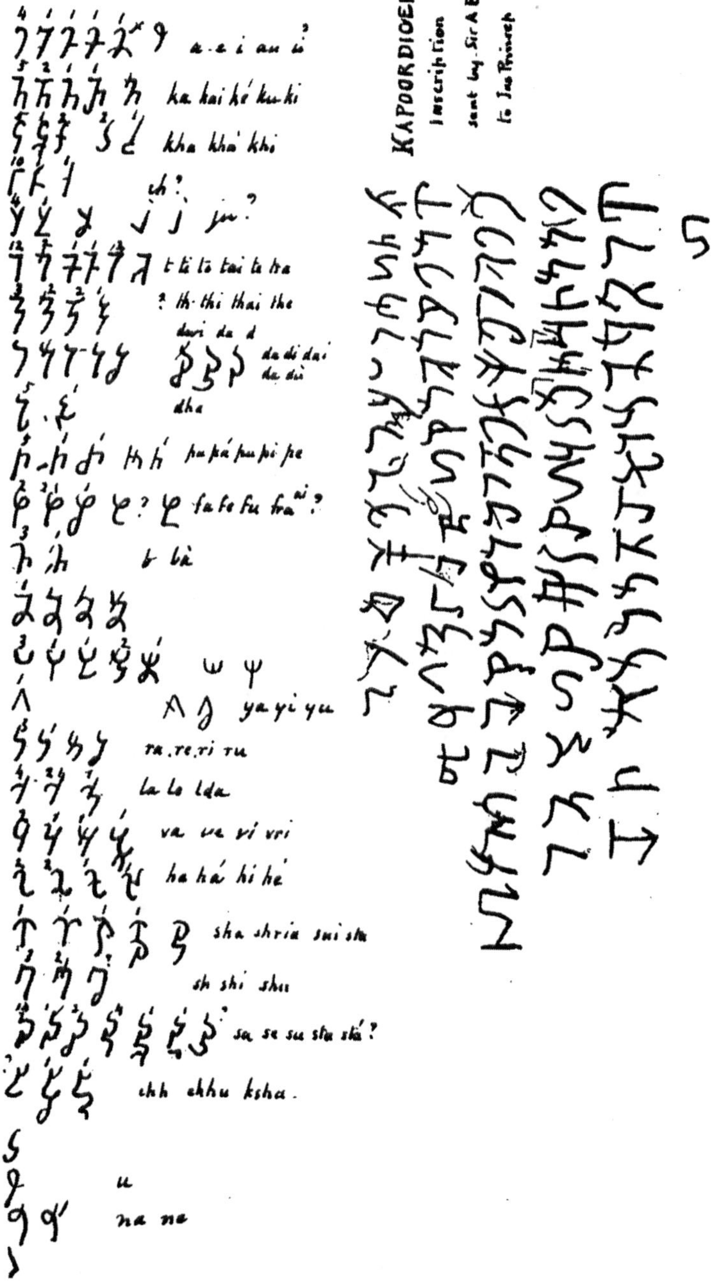